ReInventing You

Kirsten Hart

LET'S START A NEW JOURNEY
TOGETHER...

CONTENTS

Other Books By Kirsten Hart

Baby Girl Murphy
Chat
Chat Teens
Chat Christmas
Kirsten Hart's Beauty Secrets

www.KirstenHart.com

A Lifelong Journey

Queen Esther in the Bible is always portrayed as a bit of a Pageant Queen that happened to be picked at the right time by the King (because of her rare beauty), and was given the title of Queen over the land just in time to spare the Israelites from complete annihilation. She's always been the biblical poster child for God changing your life suddenly, when you least expect it, and turning you into a Princess/Queen. *'If he can take an ordinary Hebrew girl, and make her Queen, just think what he can do with your life."*

Were it only that simple and pretty. Recently, I did quite a bit of research on Esther for a retreat I spoke for in Anaheim, California. It was a great church. Sweet, sweet, ladies. They had tiaras and boas for all the women to wear, with the retreat theme of God changing us all into beautiful Queens. And it should seem that simple, right? After all, we are told in the Bible that Esther went through a whole *year* of *beauty treatments.* A girl's dream come true. Who wouldn't want that?

Unfortunately, her story isn't so pretty. Do you remember the story? It's very soap opera-ish. Queen Vashti (in the midst of a year and a half of entertaining drunken strangers in her home) was summoned by King Ahasuerus to appear (it is traditionally believed) completely nude before all of the drunk male guests, wearing only her crown. She refuses, and is banished (presumably killed). King Ahasuerus later regrets what he did to the queen, but can't change what was already done. So it is recommended that he bring all of the beautiful young virgins from across his empire, and choose one to be his new queen.

The ancient Jewish historian Josephus says the Ahasuerus had a total of 400 young virgins selected. It sounds wonderful – a year of constant spa treatments, etc. Yet the destiny of these women should also be considered: one evening with the king. Going 'in to' the King's chambers meant one thing: sex. And, if we're being honest: rape. These young virgin girls were taken from their families and homes for a singular reason. To see if the King found pleasure in one of them. If the woman pleasured him, she would be considered for the new title of Queen.

As for the 399 who weren't chosen after that one night, they were banished to the harem where they stayed a concubine of the king, but rarely if ever saw him afterwards. And they were never free to marry another man, essentially living as a perpetual unwanted. Because once they had been sexually defiled, law stated they were not allowed to marry another man. A lifelong sentence of being the King's concubine.

Not so pretty, huh? But yet there was purpose to Esther walking through nearly a year of preparation to 'go in to' the King's chambers. God had a bigger plan. Through the hardship of knowing your 'beauty preparations' are only for the King's pleasure for one night, God used that humiliating experience to promote Esther to a place where she could save the lives of the Israelites in King Ahasuerus' kingdom.

When hearing the story of Esther, we are rarely told about the King having sex with hundreds of virgin girls. We see Esther's story as a beautiful transformation from girl to Queen. How God reinvented her life.

ReInventing You is a book of hopes, dreams, and visions for your life. But just remember that sometimes those experiences that transform and reinvent us are harsh, and difficult to walk through. Yes, God used Esther for a greater purpose than she could have realized early on, but imagine what was going through her mind (and all of the minds of those taken virgins), as they were being taught what the King wanted from them. Not pleasant stuff. Not easy. Not *fun*.

I love instant. I love instant results from a dream God has placed in my heart. But as many of us have learned over our life's journey, God's timetable is often times vastly different from ours.

David was just a young boy in his early teens when he was anointed by Samuel to be the future King of Israel. How unbelievable for this young shepherd boy to know that he was going to be the next *king*. Yet between the time he was anointed, and the age he actually became the King, was a span of approximately fifteen years (give or take).

Some of us have dreams for our future, but David actually knew for sure that this *was* in his future. It was going to happen. But he had to wait. And *wait*. I don't think I've ever had anything happen to me that I knew for sure I was destined to do/become, and then had to continue with everyday life, wading through fifteen *years* for it to take place. And for a young man to know of his destiny, fifteen years probably felt like a lifetime.

Abraham was promised by the Lord that he and Sarah would have a son. And I have got to say, I think that it's remarkable (in an age before sonograms) that Abraham was given the *gender* of the child they would have. Yet when God told Abraham of the promise of this son, both he and his wife Sarah thought it was hilarious, and a bit outlandish. They had waited their whole lives for a child, a son to pass down their family name. And now God is telling Abraham that he would, in his old age, be reinvented not only into a father of one son, but to be the father of a nation.

There was only one way that could happen—through natural offspring. Abraham was seventy-five when God first gave him that verbal promise. Genesis chapter twelve contains the full promise God gave Abraham, that included the 'father of nations' title. There are approximately twenty-five years between the time God promised Abraham that he would 'become a great nation' to the time God gave him Isaac.

Now twenty-five years is a *long* time for anyone to wait for a promise. Especially as big a promise as God presented to Abraham. Every single year Abraham was one step further away, biologically, from the actuality of that promise coming true. To conceive at seventy-five? Sketchy. But to conceive at ninety-nine? Pretty darn near impossible. And Abraham and Sarah knew it.

But yet, from reading the scriptures, we know it happened. Miracle of miracles. God kept his promise. He always does. Sometimes it just seems *really* last minute.

Perhaps God planted a seed in your heart years ago. Something you *know that you know* God promised you. Yet you're still waiting. You just simply can't give up. Know that God is molding you to fit that dream. Reinvention is a process. The outcome is always worth the days, weeks, or years in transition.

Why did Abraham and Sarah have to wait for

twenty-five years for their promise? I have absolutely no idea. I could take guesses, but I may not be right. What I do know, is that there is reason and purpose to everyday and every step of our life journey. What we can't see through our limited vision, God sees in perfect clarity. It's not our job to make those promises come about as we see fit. Sarah did that, and Ishmael was born.

Since it seemed an impossibility that Sarah and Abraham would conceive a son at their stage in life, Sarah pressed to make God's promise come about as she saw fit. But really, we can't blame her. I have totally done the same thing. Haven't we all at times? Only Sarah's decision to have Hagar be the carrier of God's promise, is that she overstepped her place.

This might sound odd, but I'm glad we have Sarah's life to read about now. It's encouraging in a weird way, to know that we're not the only ones wanting God to move his 'reinventions' along as a quicker pace. Sarah and Abraham did it. We do it. Thousands of years apart. And the crazy thing is, we *still* do it!

Ishmael was the child born out of 'man' trying to humanly interpret God's plan and timetable. We are in a journey. A lifelong journey of searching out who God ultimately wants us to be and do throughout our lifetime. To walk out our purpose on this earth. Whether it's for us to maintain the same lifestyle and career our whole lives, or to be reinvented multiple times along the journey, only God himself, knows.

Don't create an Ishmael. Wait for your Isaac. Even if it takes a lifetime. Abraham was one hundred years old when his dream, wish, and promise came true. Are you willing to wait that long? Even if it takes your whole life?

Who you are today is probably not who you are going to be in five years, ten years, or in the golden years of your life. God will continue to stretch you, develop you, and reinvent you into more of his perfect design. Isn't that exciting? Stagnancy is for ponds. We humans are created in the likeness of our creator, and even though he doesn't change character, he is constantly creating. And our lives must reflect that character. I don't believe God created us for stagnancy, rather for evolving and creating new ways to use our giftings and abilities.

Jump in that flow of life. Grab a paddle and see what adventures God has in store for your life.

Let's *go*!

WHISTLE WHILE YOU WORK

*A strength is "an activity that makes you feel strong."
It is an activity where the doing of it invigorates you.
Before you do it, you find yourself instinctively looking
forward to it. While you are doing it you don't
struggle to concentrate, but instead you become so
immersed that time speeds up and you lose yourself
in the present moment. And after you are finished
doing it, you feel authentic, connected to the best
parts of who you really are.*
--Marcus Buckingham

Do you know the feeling? That wonderfulness when
you realize you are living right in the center of who

you were created to be? When you lose yourself in the joy of work? When it seems as if everything you were created to be is in perfect alignment with your body, mind, and soul? There is nothing like it.

A few months ago it totally happened to me. My husband Dave, our youngest son, Ryan, and I were at a Family Camp near Ruidoso, New Mexico. Have you ever been to that part of the country? It's beautiful. It's marvelous. It was such a needed break from the 100+ degree temperatures we were having at home this past summer. The average temperature in the daytime in Ruidoso? That would be 73 degrees, which is my favorite temperature. Call me odd, but I have a personal favorite temperature. It's 73 degrees with no humidity. I believe down deep that 73 will be the year-round temperature of Heaven. It's temperature's equivalent of the number 777.

We stayed in a campground chic little metal-roofed cabin complete with framed cross-stitched bible verses and woodland birds circa 1970's, and the popular sponge-painted walls of the early 1990's. Every afternoon, as if the clouds themselves had an alarm clock, we had the noon-to-2:00pm rain shower. Sometimes not so much a shower, but rather a massive downpour. Sure enough, we attempted to time our afternoons so that we would be cozily tucked under the covers of our cabin-sized bed for that miraculous rain. The windows were flung open, and the wafting scents of pine trees and fresh rain from the skies filled our slumbering nostrils. Sheer perfection. If I could properly reproduce that scent into a room spray or candle, I'd be a billionaire.

It was 112-117 degrees back home all that week. I wasn't going to return until the temperatures in my home town fell back into digits that were safe for human existence. Nope. Can't make me go back. Just send the kittens to the nearest airport, and I'd have everything I needed to spend the rest of my summer days at my little cabin in Heaven, thank you very much.

My husband was leading the music for the whole camp. I sang on his worship team, and in the choir. Two full services a day. 10am and 7pm. I never made it to the 6:30am prayer time or the 8:00am teaching time. Folks, God isn't even up at those hours in the mountains! That mountain air is good for sleeping! I had enough church that week to get me a 'free skip from church pass' for at least a month.

The pastor in charge of the whole week asked me if I would share my adoption story with everyone at the Friday morning service. I just had a 15-20 minute slot. In order to shrink my 60+minute version down to 15 minutes, I was practicing my auctioneer speed talking. *I hope they'll be able to understand me with the speed that I will be speaking.* Must make the pronunciation impeccably clear.

Friday morning came. I was wearing black. I love black. Even though it might be an optical illusion, I always feel a bit skinnier when I wear the color. Skinnier is always better. I have tossed around the idea of having a complete wardrobe of just black. Everything would be interchangeable.

Music was sung, the offering was taken, and it was my turn to be center stage. "Would you like a headset microphone?" I had been asked prior to the service. "No thank you," I responded, "I would have no idea what to do with my right hand if I wore one of those. My whole right arm would feel like a hundred pound weight that was a complete separate entity from my body if I didn't have a microphone to hold while speaking," I told the sound man, who looked at me oddly. Sound men can be a little non-humor-filled at times.

I started my story the same way I always did, except that my speaking was equivalent to a record/album/LP speed set on HIGH. Do you remember doing that? I remember taking my Partridge Family record, and paying it at high speed. They sounded like little munchkins singing 'Come On Get Happy'. Kids these days have no idea the hours of the fun that can be had sitting around your record player after school. We didn't need video games or computers back then. We had our record players, banana seat bikes, and tire swings. I'm sounding old.

I count it a treat every time I get to share my story. By simply trying to order a copy of my birth certificate at the age of forty-one, I started on a long new journey in which I discovered that I (surprise!) had been adopted. I am honored to share my story with audiences across the country.

When I get up to speak for an audience, I experience 'it'. That rush of wholeness. That coming together of who I was always created to be. Yet I never thought speaking before audiences would be my 'thing'. God completely reinvented me into a speaker.

Dave and I have been doing concerts together for over twenty-five years. I remember the days before I started speaking for groups. We'd be getting ready to go up on stage to sing, and Dave would whisper to me, "Be ready to share something. A scripture or a thought sometime during the concert." I immediately would have internal gastronomical issues. Really? He wanted me to speak and share something? Please, no. No thanks, but thank you very much. I'm just fine singing. Singing and smiling, that's what I do. You, my dear, may do all of the talking.

I was never great at memorizing scripture, so the only 'verse' that I had ready was 'Jesus wept'. Not very fitting in most Sunday concerts that we had. "Kirsten, would you share something..."

"Jesus wept".

Thank you. Curtsy. Bow. Back to singing.

If it had only been that easy.

"Hon, I really don't have anything to share. Speaking is so not my comfort zone. You're great at it.

Could you possibly not call on me to speak during our concerts." Smile. Smile. Kiss. Hug. Flirt. Wink.

Times had changed. I now had a *story!* I had something to actually say. Miracle of miracles—the girl speaks! Who knew?

There were probably 400+ people in the audience that morning. (Look who's a big girl now!) No intestinal issues, and I was actually enjoying it. I looked around as I spoke, and people were listening intently. That's always a good sign. Note to other speakers: if people are falling asleep while you're speaking, it's time to tie things up. That or talk exceptionally loud. Or thump on the pulpit. Thumping usually always works.

They were with me. They were listening. The miraculous was taking place. There's something other-worldly about getting up to speak without notes in front of you. Every time it's different. Same story, just told a little differently. "Speak through me, God. This is your story that you gave me. Use it. Speak that story through me in a fresh way today." That's usually my prayer that I quietly speak before every time I get up to share.

God faithfully shows up. Have you had that happen? When you plan one thing, perhaps even have a perfectly planned and detailed outline, and something totally different transpires, and you realize that God had an agenda better than you could ever prepare? That's good stuff. Great stuff.

All of a sudden I found myself sharing something

15

that I had never spoken on before. I hadn't planned on saying it. It just came out. A few sentences into my new thoughts, I saw the evangelist who was there for the whole week take out a pad of paper and quickly start writing. I guessed that or he had a few last minute ideas he wanted to share when he took the platform after I was done. Or was it possible that he was *taking notes on what I was saying*?

My time was up. I didn't want to go over my time limit. No one likes it when speakers do that. Be respectful of the time given, and maybe (just maybe) they'll have you back again.

When I sat back down next to my husband in the audience's indoor-outdoor white plastic seats from Walmart (that thankfully had armrests), my husband leaned over to whisper to me. "I've never heard you share that before. Great new point. Wow, babes, I loved it."

It was at that point where I realized I was fully walking in my true life's calling. It is truly a joy to have a career doing what I absolutely love. If indeed what I did by sharing my heart and sharing my stories made a positive impact on someone else's life, or encouraged them in their life walk, what greater purpose could I have?

While I was speaking, it was as if I had morphed into another realm. The twenty minutes that I spoke flowed by as if it had been mere seconds. Fresh ideas and words emitted from my mouth as melted dark chocolate flowing into a candy bar mold in

Switzerland. *(Mmmm,* chocolate.)

I was smack dab in the middle of my calling. It was that sweet spot of peace. I enjoyed every second of speaking. It was who I was created to be. But it took me years to be reinvented into being comfortable enough to *speak* in front of audiences!

When I think of Snow White singing 'Whistle While You Work', it seems the perfect song for a cartoon fairy tale. No one in real life whistles while they work. Work is aptly named. It's hard. It's not fun. No one goes around whistling songs while they're at work. It's all silliness.

What *if?* What if it were possible to live your life whistling while you worked? Work would have to be enjoyable, right? Perhaps the people who work the rides at Disney are the only ones who have a job worthy of whistling. Not the normal person. We don't enjoy work. We enjoy our weekends, because that's the only time we actually get to have fun.

Throughout this book, my hope is that you will discover who you were created to be, what you were designed to do, and how God may reinvent you. The ultimate sweet spot in life? Find what you love to do and create a way to make a living doing that very thing. Sound impossible? I'm a living, walking, (eating), and breathing example that dreams can be a reality.

Now, if you'll excuse me I need to go dig in my pantry and find some dark Swiss chocolate.

UPHILL BOTH WAYS

The nights were short. The days were long. You worked all day for a few dollars. You could hardly put enough food on the table to feed your family. And, yes, you had to walk ten miles in the snow to school barefoot, and it was uphill both ways.

I thoroughly realize that life was a lot harder 'back in the day'. I, for one, am so thankful that I wasn't born in a time when outdoor toilets were still the rage. I am thankful for inside potties. Very. Although I have heard of areas that still had outhouses in use within the past ten years. Unbelievable.

You go to school, finish high school if you're lucky, get a job, get married, have some kids, work until retirement age, and retire to Florida. You were grateful to have had a job. It was work. Lots of hard work for little pay. Suck it up, and be thankful.

That was life. Some people were fortunate enough to have *careers.* Those were the rich people. Doctors, Judges, Astronauts, College Professors, all of those in the medical field and in politics were career people. Careers were prestigious. Jobs were commonplace. Then there were those people called actors.

The actors in Hollywood were the lucky ones. They got paid the big bucks to 'play' all day. They went to big Hollywood parties. What a life. Living in Beverly Hills and enjoying all the niceties life had to offer. That kind of lifestyle was only reserved for the elite. Just a few. The rest of the world trudged through jobs. Many in factory jobs. The only goal was to receive that paycheck at the end of the week. A position in management was sometimes the only goal, but those positions were reserved for the young up-and-coming kids.

I started my job career young. I was a Brownie selling Girl Scout Cookies. My parents were teaching music at a private college prep school in Princeton, New Jersey. We, as well as most of the school staff, lived on the grounds. Such a beautiful place. My family lived in a staff apartment in the grand Russell Hall building, which was a huge family estate mansion house turned dormitory for the all-boys boarding school. Very Ivy League. Very high-brow East Coast.

I was given the daunting task, as so many before me and so many after me have had, of selling Girl Scout Cookies. This was in the early 1970's. Back when just the basic cookies were available. Back when you got a decent amount of Thin Mints in your box! Two large sleeves to be exact! Heaven in a plastic sleeve. And, oh, Thin Mints straight out of the freezer...nothing better!

Back to my selling story. Well, I was on a mission. Sell, sell, sell! There were only a few times a day when a *girl* would be allowed to enter the boy's dorms. When that hour arrived, I entered. And I sold. I knocked on every single dorm room door of every single dorm. Those rich high school boys *ordered* my cookies! They ordered so many boxes that I was the #1 seller for that season. Thank you. Thank you very much. I think I won a ribbon or something. A ribbon and the knowledge that I had beat out every other Brownie in my troupe for the #1 spot.

That next Fall, my Johnson Park Elementary School had a fund raising campaign. The campaign involved selling pre-printed Christmas cards. Trust me, they were all the rage in the early 70's. Very vogue. Basically they were Christmas cards that you could have your name, the names of all your family members, and whatever special Christmas greeting you wanted professionally printed at the bottom of the MERRY CHRISTMAS generic page. This time I had an even better selling incentive. PRIZES! And *good* prizes, mind you. Look OUT Hun School!

This time I not only hit up all the employees, staff, and teachers at the Hun School, I also canvassed every single residence in the neighborhood. My borders were the two busy streets: Lawrenceville Road and

Rosedale Road. The streets and houses in-between? All my selling territory!

I had my catalog in hand and set out. Ding-Dong. Knock-Knock. I knew these houses from Trick-or-Treating, but now I would know them in a whole new way. These were the people who would help me get those PRIZES!

I sold. And I sold. And I sold. That's right. #1 seller AGAIN, thank you very much! (As I'm writing this I'm wondering why I went into a career of singing, speaking, and writing instead of SALES...) I don't recall how many boxes of Christmas cards I sold that year, but I do remember it took me days to get them all delivered. My little, 'Hello, my name is Kirsten...' speech that I gave to open the deal making worked well.

I got some serious prize loot, too. I bought a new blender for my parents (Did they suggest that I pick that item??? My memory is failing me), a rock tumbler (very, very 1970's), jewelry making kits, and literally box loads of fun stuff! The business woman in me was born.

My parents picked up on my door-to-door selling 'giftedness'. Not too long after my Christmas card sell-a-thon, they thought to capitalize on this new selling machine of theirs. I was no longer just their child. My childhood innocence and days of playing with Barbies was gone. It was time to get out and earn my keep. I was now the newest TOILET BOWL CLEANER saleswoman in town. Yep. You read that right.

My parents bought cases of these hook-on-the-back-of-the-inside-of-your-toilet-tank blue dye cleaners. Just the perfect fit for a little 8 year-old girl to sell. 'She sold the heck out of those Christmas cards, I'm thinking this girl could sell toilet bowl cleaners like nobody's business'. My parents wrote my sales pitch on a 3 x 5 index card. "Take this and memorize it", I was told. This wasn't seeming as fun as a selling Christmas cards that had a whole brochure full of prizes you could win. My parents handed me no such potential prize list. No rock tumbling or jewelry making kits as incentives. Just an index card. An index card with a lot of words on it to memorize.

I was a good girl. I memorized my pitch. I adjusted the right inflections for certain words that my parents coached me with. "Now go to our front door and pretend we are someone you are giving the pitch to". When I had the "Hello, my name is..." speech down pat, I was off. I had a whole case of toilet bowl cleaners to sell that afternoon, with more sitting in our basement.

I guess something about my "Please buy these strange objects from me" look worked. It worked well enough that after the cases of toilet bowl cleaners were sold, my parents thought I was ready for an upgrade. I was upgraded from inside the tank toilet bowl cleaners to sit-on-top-of-the-tank-lid glass domed plastic flower-filled room fresheners. If you lived in the 70's you will probably remember these.

On the road a few years ago, when staying in a host home, I almost fainted when I saw one of MY glass flowered room fresheners sitting on TOP OF THEIR TOILET! Just how many years had that thing been sitting there? Unbelievable.

If I remember correctly, these fancy fresheners were available in three scents, and multiple plastic flower-colored looks. They had vitamin E looking capsules in the bottom, that you would prick with a pin to make the scent come out stronger. These were a little harder to tote door-to-door than the toilet tank cleaners. I was a little girl working with glass containers. Really mom and dad? *Really?*

I received a new 3 x 5 with yet another pitch to memorize. Once again, I went outside of our front door and worked the speech with my parents, who for all acting and selling purposes weren't my 'parents', but rather neighbors who were potential customers. When I got the thumbs up that I was prepared enough to hit the neighborhood, I was a selling machine. I'm thinking at this point the neighbors were being sweet, and participating in 'pity buys'. "Maybe if we buy enough of these bathroom fresheners, this poor little girl won't be sent out anymore."

After I hit up every neighbor within walking distance, my parents got the genius idea to expand my territory. "We're going to drop you off here, and we'll pick you up again in two hours." It was just me and two cases of plastic flowered fresheners. A new neighborhood. New people. New bathrooms that needed to be scented. I just wanted to be home eating some cookies and playing with my Barbie pop-up camper and jeep.

I am seriously amazed that I wasn't abducted during those months. I know there wasn't as much talk of abductions in those days, but honestly, I was just a little girl! A little girl walking around with glass and plastic flowered bathroom deodorizers and a manila envelope filled with cash. I'm thinking I may need some therapy right now. Anyone available? Text me your number.

The awful thing is, I don't recall keeping much of the toilet bowl cleaner or bathroom scenter money? I suppose it went towards clothes and food! I 'earned my keep' in those days. See, I know what hard work is! Perhaps I didn't have to slave away in coal mines, but for goodness sake, I was a young girl peddling my wares around foreign neighborhoods! And for additional pity emphasis, I played the cello in fourth and fifth grade, and I walked over a mile to and from school carrying that huge instrument! Pity? Any pity votes coming my way?

Eventually the toilet and bathroom products were all sold, and my first 'real' job was working in the cafeteria at my high school. I was what they called a 'day student', while most of the people attending The Pennington School were boarders. Again, very east coast. On Saturdays, I worked in the cafeteria for breakfast, lunch, and dinner. I think I made probably $35 a Saturday, which was nice extra money that I kept for myself this time.

The goal of an actual career lay ahead of me. If I went to college and studied hard, I could make money doing what I loved. I was given a different school of thought than the generations before me. Times had changed!

Today gobs of professional athletes are paid outrageous salaries for 'playing' their sports. The billionaires of today are those who have come up with original ideas, marketed those ideas, and enjoy what they do. 'Find a problem and solve it' is the key to success. The people who sat and tinkered for fun in their garages are turning those creations into the world's greatest money makers. Life isn't all about all work and no play. Video game designers play all day, and get paid millions of dollars to do so!

It's a whole new world, my friends. You are just one creative and innovative thought away from being a millionaire. Seriously! Isn't that exciting?

I've always been searching for my possible million dollar idea. And I've had a few. My best? Why, that would be Meal Scented Candles! You'll be wishing you had been the first one to come up with this fantastic idea. Trust me. It's pure genius.

Now here's how I thought up the candle idea. I walked into our home one afternoon when a roast was cooking in the crock pot. Is that not just one of the best smells in the world? Agree with me here. It's comforting, it makes a house smell like a home, and the anticipation of a wonderful meal awaiting you is second to none. Now, who wouldn't want to reproduce that intoxicating scent anytime they wanted?

My mind started racing. Lasagna scented, chicken soup scented, BBQ scented, Thanksgiving dinner scented, and the list went on! What if I divided the candles into three separate sections? Say, perhaps for the Thanksgiving Meal Candle, I have one section that smelled like turkey basting, another that smelled like sweet potato casserole, and a third that replicated homemade yeast rolls. I bet you're getting hungry just reading this! See...great idea, huh!

"Dave," I called to my husband, "I totally have our money making idea! Oprah is so going to have this on her Favorite Things show next year!"

I got brainstorming. I could market these candles to anyone, but especially bachelors and non-cookers. What bachelor wouldn't want to bring home a date with his house smelling like a fresh baked Italian dinner, and then pull out a Stouffer's lasagna out of the oven? It would smell like he had been baking all day (especially with the Lasagna/Garlic Bread/Fettuccine Trio Candle burning). The ideas were flowing non-stop. Yeah, this was great money making stuff. And believe me, from my days of going door-to-door, I could spot a good money maker a mile away.

I brainstormed as any good inventor does. I wrote down on paper my brilliant trio candle scents. No more debt for this family. Trips, new cars, and large houses lay in wait for our future. This was IT.

It was getting late in the evening, but my mind was racing. It was time to make my test product. Time to create my baby. It was as if I were Dr. Frankenstein (which, if you recall, was actually the name of the scientist in the movie who created the monster, not the name of the monster) and I was about to bring life to this new creature of mine. Muwaa-haa-haa-haaa (evil laugh). Time to run to Walmart for supplies.

Michael's and Hobby Lobby were my first choices for meal scented candle making supplies, but at this time of night, they were both closed already. Walmart it was. 11pm and I was on my way. Craziness, I know, but when an idea is birthing inside of you, you need to seize the moment! Take note.

The last time I had created a candle was in Mrs. Papp's 4th grade class at Lore Elementary. We were studying the American Revolutionary War, and a special guest came into our classroom to teach us the fine art of candle making. Mrs. Papp would be proud of me (God rest her soul, if she's even still alive after all these years) that I was attempting to relive that candle making experience. If I recall correctly, I believe the woman who taught us to 'dip...now dip again...and again...' was wearing Revolutionary War appropriate clothing. Some of the reenactors take that stuff way too seriously.

What did I need? Glass jars. Check. String. Check. A pencil to tie the string to at the top of the jar. Check. Now wax. No wax chips in the craft section at this Walmart. Hobby Lobby would have made this all the much easier. Dang. I put my thinking cap on and headed to the candles section. I found some unscented white candle tapers. Perfect. Well, perfect enough for the experiment for tonight. I would have to order wax chips in bulk for the future. Did they sell them that way? I would search that out in the morning.

Now for the first of my scents. Which meal did I want to recreate for my first (of many) Meal Candles. Drum roll, please. Actually, it was getting close to midnight, and Dr. Frankenstein-a was starting to get sleepy. Let's get on with this...

I went to the spices aisle. I looked at what they had. It was time for the genius to kick in. What meal could I reproduce from these spices in front of me? I saw the chicken bouillon cubes. A-ha. Chicken soup. Thank you genius part of my brain. Perfect. I bought bouillon cubes and a special chicken and garlic seasoning. You have got to start somewhere. A Chicken Soup Candle was my somewhere. Oh, Oprah, you are so going to love these!

It was after midnight when I started to melt my non-scented candles into a Dutch oven on top of my stove. Go ahead, just call me the Pioneering Revolutionary Woman of the West. I was feeling organic. I was feeling 'pionneery'. I would have fit right in with the characters on Little House on the Prairie. Wait, that's a different era than the Revolutionary War. But you get my idea. I was transported back to a simpler time. When women honed their candle making skills. I was a vision of the past living in the 21st century.

I melted my wax. I sprayed PAM into the glass jar (the poor pioneer women didn't have the advantage of having PAM available back then). I added my special seasonings to the wax. Trust me, you could have pulled out a spoon and started slurping away. That candle wax was the sipping image (instead of spitting image...sipping image...my attempt at being punny...) of a bowl of homemade chicken noodle!

It was getting late. I was getting very sleepy. I poured the scented wax in the glass jar, attached the measured string around the pencil, and carefully laid the pencil across the rim of the jar. Mrs. Papp would have been proud. I would have received an A for that project.

I cleaned up a bit, and left the rest for the morning. I was the last one still awake. Everyone was already deep into their REM sleep cycle. I brushed my teeth and turned out the lights. It had been a full day. Tomorrow I would unveil my million dollar money maker. This was my last night to sleep as a middle class citizen. I'll need to invest in higher thread count sheets in a few weeks...

Morning came. My husband woke up. "What's that SMELL???" were the first words out of his mouth? I sniffed. I smelled it, too. "That's my Chicken Noodle Soup Meal Candle. I made it last night while you were sleeping!"

My enthusiasm didn't last long. I took my husband

by the hand and led him downstairs to view my creation. Every step of descent brought the now slightly pungent odor more alive. The couches, curtains, and every porous material in the house had grasped hold of the waxy chicken and garlic scent. It wasn't good, my friends. It's not a scent you want in your house first thing in the morning, It's probably not a scent you would ever want in your home for that matter.

I so wanted to burn the candle. Yet I so wanted to keep my marriage intact. There's a reason candle companies sell candles with the scents of pumpkin, apple, and cinnamon. They are pleasing scents. They smell good anytime of the day. My attempt at recreating chicken soup into a wax product was a complete failure. Just like Dr. Frankenstein realized when his monster killed that little girl. Some things just aren't meant to be created. Some creations are better left in an uncreated state.

Oprah wouldn't be calling me. I would still have to be paying a mortgage and car payment, and my sheet thread counts would remain in the low hundreds. It was a good idea. If I just had a chemist who was a friend, and would be willing to work up a chemical equivalent of a turkey dinner without the ingredients of bouillon cubes, my idea STILL MAY WORK!

I'm not giving up. Perhaps one day you will walk into your local card and gift store, and think, "Hmmm, who's cooking homemade BBQ?" only to realize it is my CANDLE sitting on the table in front of you! A girl can still dream, can't she?

True, not every road to success is easy. You may end up having to walk barefoot in snow for miles uphill for years, but somewhere along the road, it has to take a turn. Spring comes, the snow melts, you find a pair of shoes, the road gets paved, and it starts to gently slope downward. We, at this time in our world have every opportunity to succeed in front of us. The world truly is your oyster. As Walt Disney stated, 'If you can dream it, You can do it'.

Don't give up on your dreams. Don't think all you will ever be able to do in life is just work a job, and never actually have a career doing something you love. Why those years of me selling weird bathroom accessories? Perhaps, because as a speaker and author, I am self-employed. My 'product'? *Me.* It may sound odd, but in order to get speaking engagements, I have to '*sell* me'. And those years of door-to-door sales gave me the confidence to sell! (Thanks, Mom and Dad)

Is your life just a job? Do you love what you do? Can you see your present employment as a tool that God is using to bring you into a new place in your life? Or does your day-to-day make you feel as if you are literally walking to and from 'school' uphill both ways. Uphill *both* ways? Come on, that just doesn't even make sense!

FIREMEN AND BALLERINAS

I took a poll of my friends yesterday. 'Guys and Girls that grew up in the 1970's, what did you want to be when you grew up?' was the question I asked. These friends of mine are an interesting bunch. I received quite the variety of answers.

GIRLS:
Airline Stewardess, Wonder Woman, Teacher, Mom, a Grocery Clerk at Piggly Wiggly, Nurse, Singer, Dental Hygienist, Married to a Preacher, Nurse in Africa, A Missionary to Africa (which is interesting, because that's usually what people fear God will call them to once they've become a Christian!), Cosmetologist, Secretary, Fashion Designer, and Dorothy Hamill were just a few of the answers.

GUYS:
Professional Baseball Player, Batman, Preacher, Singer, owner of a Music Store, Fireman, and Funeral Director (although I have a funny feeling someone listed that last one as a joke).

Obviously, I had more women respond to my question. I don't have run-of-the-mill acquaintances. I'm sure the average elementary school student in the 1970's didn't wanted to be a preacher, but these are my friends. You should meet them someday. They keep me entertained.

I recall my own days in the early elementary grades. While the majority of my little female friends either wanted to be nurses or ballerinas, I most likely fell into the third most popular future career for little girls, and in particular little girls who loved animals. My future career would find me a veterinarian. I did indeed loved animals of all shapes, sizes, and fluffiness levels.

My goal in being a full-time veterinarian was to be able to earn enough money to buy a huge farm, and go rescue all of the stray cats and dogs of every humane society, and bring them to live forever in peace, harmony, and safety on my farm. The End.

Well, that dream did in fact end. It ended with the stark realization that in order to be a veterinarian, I would have to administer shots to animals. Even if they were to make them healthy, I couldn't see myself giving shots, because I, myself, hated them. How could I have a career doing something I hated, even though I would be able to work with animals every day? That dream died, but new ones inevitably took its place.

Boys, on the other hand had some very grand aspirations for their futures. Cowboys, astronauts, the President of the United States, GI Joe, Batman and other Superheroes were common goals of many little boys. Not many children said that when they grew up, they just wanted to make ends meet and bring in a paycheck large enough to cover that month's bills and expenses. No, they dreamed big, and spoke from their hearts.

I believe who we are created to be, and our personal career calling, is placed within us from the time we are inside of our mother's womb. God looks at each individual embryo, and pours specific giftings and talents into each of us. No two are given the same ingredients for identical gifts.

Ephesians 2:10 says, 'For we are God's workmanship, created in Christ Jesus to do good works, which God prepared in advance for us to do.' God already prepared you for a specific vocation. I love the definition for the word vocation: A strong feeling of suitability for a particular career or occupation. Where do you find that 'strong feeling of suitability'? I believe it's already deep within you, placed there by the Creator himself.

I came across a portion of scripture that leapt out

at me concerning who we are and the gifts and abilities we have within us. It's a classic case of 'I've read that Bible verse a gazillion times, and it never meant anything to me until that one time'.

The passage is found in Exodus 35: 30-35. "Then Moses said to the Israelites, "See, the LORD has chosen Bezalel son of Uri, the son of Hur, of the tribe of Judah, and he has filled him with the Spirit of God, with wisdom, with understanding, with knowledge and with all kinds of skills— to make artistic designs for work in gold, silver and bronze, to cut and set stones, to work in wood and to engage in all kinds of artistic crafts. And he has given both him and Oholiab son of Ahisamak, of the tribe of Dan, the ability to teach others. He has filled them with skill to do all kinds of work as engravers, designers, embroiderers in blue, purple and scarlet yarn and fine linen, and weavers—all of them skilled workers and designers."

Now, when I was attending Christian college, and had to read the entire Old Testament as part of my Introduction to the Old Testament class, I fell asleep reading many of these types of passages. B-O-R-I-N-G. Boring until you discover that what you're reading can relate to your life. Now you may have to dig a bit to see why I included this verse, but I think it's a gem!

First off, I love Moses. He's my favorite person in the Bible. (Other than Jesus, of course. He's a given.) I love the relationship that Moses had with God. He could be honest and open with his creator. I think God really liked Moses' candid nature. Moses didn't hold back his feelings with God, and God could handle it. Perhaps I need to write a book about all the qualities I love about Moses.

So God was giving Moses all kinds of inside scoop on what he wanted and needed. Moses was his #1 go-to man to get things done. It was time to create the Ark of the Covenant, and I would be putting it mild to say that God was being specific in what he wanted. This God of ours is a detailed creator! God himself tells Moses who he wants to craft the Ark's details. There's just something that I love when God calls out Bezalel.

He knows him. God knows him well. 'Bezalel, son of Uri, son of Hur, tribe of Judah'. God specifies his ancestry, as well as his address. I'm sorry, that just makes me smile. God knows your specifics. He knows everything about you and I. "You know Kirsten, daughter of Greg, birth daughter of Gary, at 9208 Branson Landing Blvd." I admire his detailed descriptions!

Moses tells the 'congregation' that God filled Bezalel with the Spirit of God (which is interesting, because the Holy Spirit hadn't been dispersed to humans yet...only in individual cases), and filled him with 'skill, ability, and know-how for making all sorts of things'. Then God goes on to describe in detail the skills Bezalel has, and ends with the fact that he is also gifted in every kind of skilled craft, including teaching!

God then lists some more very specific things that Bezalel and his friend, Oholiab (such different names back then) are gifted in. Really specific details!

Don't let these verses fly by. They're so good! God knows your ancestry, your address, *and* every tiny detail of talent he has put into you! He knows his creations by name! He hasn't forgotten what he placed inside of you from the very beginning of your creation. What you're good at? God put that in you! What you love to do, and have discovered you can do well? He gave you those abilities. You're not just some random creation. You are designed for a purpose. Our job is to live our lives using up every last drop of ability.

On a Saturday afternoon this past summer, while it was boiling outside, I enjoyed an afternoon of watching some of Oprah's last shows. She had a show where she showed clips from some of her favorite guests. One of her absolute favorites, was a little boy named Mattie Stepanek. Mattie appeared on the Oprah show many times over her last decade. He wrote many New York Times best-selling books, gave speeches across the country, and raised millions for MDA.

Watching the show, I heard a sentence that Mattie spoke to his mother as he was in his last days of life. "Have I done enough?" He was thirteen years old when he died. He had influenced Presidents and people across the world, yet he wanted to know if he had 'done enough' in his short life. Had he fulfilled everything he was meant to do while alive on this planet.

How many of us ask that of ourselves? Have I done enough? Have I done enough with what God has given me? You're probably well past the age that Mattie was when he passed on. Knowing that God is the giver of your talents, have you done enough with what he's placed inside of you? Have I done enough? I ask myself the same question. A question worth asking ourselves year after year.

Somewhere between the elementary school playground and the time we take our first job out of college, the ballerina shoes are set in a storage box, and the astronaut helmet is sold at a garage sale. The hopes and dreams we had in our innocent years are replaced with the more grounded realization that you should be grateful to even find a place that would hire you. Life isn't so much about what you would love to *be* someday, it's more about making a paycheck and putting food on the table. Dreams are for the young. This is real life.

In middle school, I went with my parents to see a married couple give a concert at a church in town. Their names were Denny and DeAnza Duron. Denny was a semi well-known football player. He and his wife were just gorgeous. They sang together. As I watched them sing together on stage, a new dream was born. I had a new vision of what I want to be when I 'grew up'. I wanted to be the Durons! I wanted to travel and sing with a handsome husband, just like DeAnza. Forget Veterinary School. I wanted to sing and travel! Well, I also wanted to be in commercials, but I was pretty sure I would be able to combine both those careers quite smoothly.

That dream continued. After I graduated from college, I toured with a USO sponsored group called Re-Creation.

Our group performed shows in Veterans Administration hospitals across the country. We would personally visit all of the patients, and the literally wheel most of them down to see the show. When we weren't at a VA, we were busy doing convention shows to raise support for the VA work we did. We also had a church program. We were busy. We traveled the country. I loved it.

The only thing missing was that gorgeous singing husband. I always assumed that I would get engaged during the last year of college, and journey into my newly graduated life a married woman. I thought an MRS degree went hand-in-hand with a BS degree. As I found out, good things really do come to those that wait.

After a year with the USO group, my parents told me about a gospel group that had an opening for a female singer. That group was called Eternity. I had been with Re-Creation a whole year, when the group Eternity was nearby in concert. We actually had a day off, so I went to both hear their concert as well as audition for them. I hate auditioning. Is that awful? You are nervous, and never do as well as 'normal' because you are being judged for that one song you sing. Not my comfort zone!

My good friend from Re-Creation went with me. While we were parking the car, I saw this version of my ultimate Dream Man step outside of Eternity's bus, and get his luggage out of the bins. He took my breath away. You know how you have this image of exactly what you want your spouse to look like? Well, he was it. Down to every last detail.

We got out of the car, and at this point, there were hundreds of butterflies in my stomach. Butterflies for this impending vocal audition, as well as my anticipation for meeting this Dream Man of mine. I walked up to the bus and introduced myself to him. B-I-N-G-O. This man was the vocal director for the group. The head honcho. The man in charge. I liked that. I liked him immediately. He even dressed really well. Stop the presses, I had found my ideal man.

He led my friend and I into the parsonage where the rest of the group was having dinner. After introducing me to everyone, he excused himself. He was going upstairs to take a shower and get ready for the concert. I immediately missed him as he vanished behind the railing. What was happening with me?

The concert was great. I couldn't keep my eyes of this vocal director. He was 'Denny'. He was what I imagined my Denny Duran to be. I could be his DeAnza. My middle school dream of singing and touring with my future husband was fleshing itself out before my very eyes.

This vocal director had me sing Amazing Grace. It was the 1980's. That's just the song everyone used for any kind of audition. "I would like to ask you a few questions", this vocal director asked during my audition time. I was prepared to say "Yes. Yes, I will marry you if you ask me right now. Now about the ring..."

He asked me questions of what I had done vocally over the years, and then I got bold, and thought to ask him a few questions myself. "Where do you see *yourself* in five years" came out of my mouth.

"Well, I'd love to be married. My dream has always been to have a bus or motor home, and travel doing concerts with my wife and family."

What? Could this be? This has always been MY dream! Well, only my dream after the whole veterinarian dream died. Look at this man. He is physically everything I adore, and now we share the same dream?

When he told me his potential future life scenario, I thought to myself, *'Don't you dare tell him that is your dream, too. That would scare him away faster than speeding bullet. Be wise...'*

I restrained myself from telling him all about Denny and DeAnza Duron, and the fact that if he married me, he would be helping to fulfill a life-long dream that I had. Look who's getting all grow'd up! Such a big girl now!

Well, my friends, I met Dave Hart twenty-six years ago as he interviewed me for Eternity's singing position, and we have enjoyed nearly twenty-five years of the most romantic-filled, singing-filled, traveling-filled, motor home living-filled, child-raising filled years a girl could dream for. And for that ring? Heart-shaped and beautiful! Heart/Hart. Cute, huh!

Trust me, singing and touring with my hubby has been way more fulfilling than neutering and spaying cats and dogs would have ever been! God placed within me a dream that would 'use up' the giftings that he poured into my embryonic DNA. He made me who I am, in order that I would fulfill my calling and purpose for living.

Who did you always want to be? What did you always dream of doing with your life? Perhaps if your dream has not been fulfilled, you can take those ballerina slippers out of the attic and try them on again. Stick your son's astronaut helmet on your head. Remember that feeling of adventure? That thrill of 'what could be'? It's not too late. All of those dreams are still inside of you. It's time to bring them alive again. Perhaps it's time for you to reinvent your life to fulfill those childhood dreams you still carry in your heart.

No Talent
Tillie And Tom

I was going to title this chapter 'No Talent Tillie', but I want men to feel comfortable reading this book, too, and I didn't want them to feel left out. So I added the name Tom into my chapter title. Now if your name just happens to be Tillie or Tom, I sure don't want you to think that I'm implying that you don't have any talent. The Tillie and Tom names came out of nowhere. Just appeared in my brain. It just sounded kind of fun. I'll now get on to the real point of this chapter.

Perhaps you think you're a No Talent Tillie (or Tom). You aren't singing before thousands of people, or on TV, or in the movies, or flying to space, or changing the political system, or creating Meal

Candles (sorry...just had to throw that one in the mix). Your name hasn't been in lights, and no one really notices you. You blend in. You're insignificant in the world's eyes. You're nothing special.

Well, (cue fanfare music) I'm here to tell you differently. (Play fanfare music) You are a Child of the King! You are significant! You are important! You *do* make a difference in this world! You matter! You were born for greatness.

Now, don't get me wrong here. I'm not implying that if you work a 9-5 job making minimum wage, that you aren't important. Not everyone is created to be in the movies, or on TV. The world is full of people influencing the world and using every ounce of their giftedness in what some people would call mundane careers. It's all in the attitude. It's all in your approach to life. It's all in how you see your life making a difference in this world.

So we have this guy at our local Taco Bell. There's only one Taco Bell in the town we are living in right now. The Harts are Taco Bell connoisseurs. I'll never forget the first time our oldest son, Tyler, ordered his very first 'meximelt with no pico sauce' on his very own. We gave him a dollar and some change, and he could barely see over the metal counter (he's not extraordinarily short, it was just when he was much younger). It was dear and near to my heart. My baby, ordering his own meximelt. Some moments stay in your heart forever. Ah...sweet Taco Bell.

Getting back to this guy at our local Taco Bell. Last

summer was our first summer here. We had just moved every last belonging to this new town of ours. What was our dinner of choice? You guessed it, 'the Bell'. We were using the drive-thru, and the voice from the 'ORDER HERE' box surprised us. That was an interesting woman's voice, we all thought. We pulled around to the 'PAY HERE' window, and a man was standing there. That was odd. Perhaps a separate woman takes the orders, and this is just the cashier guy. When I was handing this window guy my debit card, I learned that my assumption was wrong. This indeed was the same voice that took my order. Hmm, what an interesting voice!

As life would have it, we continued to frequent this Taco Bell establishment. We were always greeted by the same voice. Now, to be honest, yes, we had a few giggles over the odd matching of the voice with the body. But here's the deal: we were ALWAYS greeted with the most positive, upbeat greetings whenever we pulled next to the 'ORDER HERE' box. The 'Welcome to Taco Bell' was enthusiastic. There was excitement behind the taking of every order. I enjoyed giving this man my order. It made me smile.

It took me a few weeks to realize that this employee was what schools term 'special'. But he was my favorite employee there. He had a job, and performed his role at 100% all the time! I loved him for it! I enjoy going to Taco Bell because of his excellent service. He is an example to those who work at fast food establishments. If everyone fulfilled their job roles to the extent that our Taco Bell man does, it could change the whole industry.

A few weeks ago, we went through the line, but another voice greeted us. *What?* Our guy wasn't working that day??? It just didn't seem right to order from someone else. Our Taco Bell run didn't seem complete. It felt wrong.

We were talking about this guy with our son Ryan's girlfriend, and she said that people post about our Taco Bell guy on a website about our town! I guess we're not the only family that thinks he's a fantastic employee! I love it. A 'No Talent Tom' he isn't! Hey, he made it into this book! He indeed did have a talent. He was exceptional in customer service. He made us happy to go to Taco Bell.

"But, Kirsten, you don't understand, I really don't have anything that I'm good at."

OK, if you feel that way, we need to work though a few things first. Come, lay down on this couch here. There ya go. That's right. Relax. Do you need a sip of water? That's good. Close your eyes. Now let's go back to your childhood.

The people I meet that feel as if they don't have any talent, or that there isn't anything special about them, grew up in environments where they were told that exact thing. Perhaps you heard some of these following lines as you were growing up:

You're too fat.
You're too skinny.

You're too tall.
You're too short.
You're not smart enough.
You're not pretty enough.
You're not handsome enough.
You can't.
You won't
No one in your family ever has, and neither will you.
Just deal with it.
You're not talented.
Where'd you come from?
We never wanted you in the first place.
You're nothing but a loser.
You're good for nothin'.
Don't expect anything out of life.
People like us don't become rich and famous.
You'll never amount to much.
You'll never make it out of this town.
Your dad/mom was a loser, and you'll be one too.

I could go on and on, but it's hard even writing those words. Do you feel like you were the only one who heard words like that? Don't. People across the world have had those ugly words directed at them for thousands of years. If you fall into that category, you are in the company of greatness. Even though those words for the most part are painful to hear, and affect the psyche down deep, you can rise above them. You can prove them wrong. Albert Einstein did! And if he can do it, you can, too!

At the age of ten, Albert Einstein began attending the school at Luitpold Gymnasium. Although he was bright in school, his Greek teacher spoke the words, "You will never amount to anything" to him. Could you imagine? I hope that horrible teacher lived enough years to see who Albert turned out to be. Talk about needing to take words back!

After 'high school' (he was in Europe, so the schooling years were a bit different from our typical high school years here in the States), he applied to Zurich Polytech in Switzerland. How did he do? He FAILED his entrance exam!

Without Albert Einstein, we would never have known the theory of relativity (which, quite honestly I still don't really understand), Quantum mechanics (there's a reason why I'm a speaker and not a scientist), the Photoelectric Effect, The Brownian Movement, the Atomic Theory of Matter, and most importantly, WHY THE SKY IS BLUE.

Some of you science junkies will understand everything that I just wrote. To me, it's all gibberish. To be honest, I'm not even really sure what gibberish is, but I'm fairly sure I used the term correctly.

The point of all of this? Albert Einstein was one of the greatest minds to have ever walked on the planet earth. Pure genius. Yet, if he had believed what his Greek teacher said about him, he would never have come into his purpose for being alive. That purpose? To confuse so many high school students who had to study and memorize his theories in Physics classes!

(Just kidding, you smarty-pants science brainiacs.)

I'm starting to feel out of my comfort zone. Science classes weren't my forte in school. I liked English better. Recess was the best. I have now regressed to my elementary school brain. OK, if I'm going there, Art was actually my favorite class. In particular when we were able to play with papier-mâché. The polar opposite of quantum physics.

Albert Einstein wasn't the only famous person to rise above what people told them. Abraham Lincoln, our sixteenth President of the United States, grew up exceptionally poor.

Abraham was born in a tiny log cabin with no window or a floor. His father could not read and hated to work. Abraham only had one year of schooling. His mother died when he was eight years old. His father remarried, and his new stepmother was the one responsible for teaching Abraham how to read. Reading was the key. It opened up a whole new world of possibilities for him.

Although he was strong and very personable, Abraham didn't come from the background you would expect for President of the United States of America. Although he was uneducated and poor, he rose above his circumstances, and became one of the most well-known and respected presidents we have ever had.

Never think that your previous circumstances determine who you will become. God can reinvent even those who have been told they would amount to nothing. Don't believe the lies that if neither of your parents succeeded that you will follow in their same footsteps. You're not a No-Talent Tillie or Tom. You were created for greatness. You can become the first in your family to succeed. Perhaps you are the next President of the United States! Now don't laugh. You never know!

OK, so now you're beginning to realize that you may actually be a TALENTED Tillie or Tom! Welcome to this side of the fence! It's nice over here. This is the side where you realize that you do have talents and gifts. You can make a difference in this world. You were created to do something extraordinary with your life.

Pull up a chair and sit for a spell. Sweet Tea? Lemonade? Scones? Come and sit with me on this new 'Porch of Potential'. We have both rocking chairs and Adirondack chairs available for your relaxing pleasure. Put your feet up. Get comfortable, you're going to like it here. Ahhh, isn't the breeze just delightful? Another scone?

"But Kirsten, I really don't have any special talents." Dear, dear one. Yes you do! Perhaps you just haven't uncovered what you're so good at yet. "More sweet tea?" Let's chat for a while. Mama Kirsten will help you unveil who you were always destined to be. This is gonna be fun.

First, let's get cleaned up. Let's wash our hands of all the negativity you've ever heard your whole life. Of course, words are hard to scrub away. It may take some time. We've got time. Now get a cool clean washcloth and wipe that sweat and dirt off your face.

There. See it now? See that beautiful face! God created that face, and I believe he actually smiled when he formed your nose, mouth, cheek bones, and beautiful expressive eyes. Why, look at them sparkling!

Now get back in your chair. Isn't it beautiful out today? Why I believe the old thermometer on the porch is reading 73°. (Wink, wink). Such a perfect non-humid temperature with the sun shining warm. OK, Darling, let's find *you*.

THE SECRET INGREDIENTS

I really do love cooking and baking. I have been quite the cookbook collector over the years. My favorites? The ones from churches. You know, when women's auxiliaries or 'circles' have decided to combine all of the church's best recipes over the past 150 years into a spiral bound collections of favorites? Friends, if you find those kinds of cookbooks at garage sales, grab them up. They're chock full of seriously the best recipes you will ever find.

I had so many recipe books, that a few years ago during a move, I decided to narrow down my collection. Talk about a pain equivalent to pulling out your nails! To choose between my 'babies'? How could a loving mother do that? They were all my beloved children.

Of course, the church cookbooks made the 'keep'

pile. My book on Authentic Chinese Cooking had never been used, although the thought that one day I would create authentic Chinese cuisine for my family of four was still intriguing. 'Sell' pile it went. Who am I kidding? I couldn't even pronounce the majority of ingredients in that book. Squid Soup? No thanks.

The save and sell process was excruciatingly long. Yes, no, maybe? The books with the simple ingredient dinners and desserts were all kept. They were more my style. The easier the better. The book full of dessert recipes that simply used a box of cake mix as the foundation for every recipe was so totally kept. I love that book. Have you ever made chocolate-chip cookies from a box cake mix? You'd love 'em. So easy and good. I'll send you the recipe.

You want it now?

Just take a box of cake mix. ANY flavor you would like. Combine the cake mix with ½ cup of butter melted and 2 eggs. A little splash of vanilla for good measure? Sure! That is your cookie base. Next add any fun ingredients you wish, or just stick with plain perfection: chocolate-chips. Bake at 350° for 10 minutes. You will thank me later.

I recently read an article written by Anne Beiler. She is the founder of Auntie Anne's Pretzels. If you have never devoured one of her famous pretzels, you are missing out on one of the best reasons to be grateful you are alive at this point and time in human history. They. Are. Delicious. I have had many for my lunch. That's right. Just a pretzel for lunch. I don't live with my mommy and daddy anymore. If I want to eat only a pretzel for lunch, I can. One of the perks of being a grown up.

In this article, Anne was telling the story of how her pretzel empire was born. She was raised in the Amish-Mennonite community of Lancaster, Pennsylvania. I remember going there as a child. I always loved the Shoo-Fly Pie. Oooh, and the homemade breads were out of this world.

In order to support her husband's vision of being a counselor, Anne bought a concession stand at a local farmer's market. They sold all kinds of foods, including fresh-rolled pretzels. All the other foods were selling well, except for the pretzels. She was contemplating removing the pretzels from their menu.

When talking with her husband about deleting the pretzels, he mentioned that an aunt of his had made delicious pretzels when he was growing up, and perhaps Anne could talk with his aunt about her pretzel recipe. They indeed tried the new recipe, and the pretzels have since become literally world famous!

Anne was close to actually taking the pretzels off the menu! Now, whenever you hear the words Auntie Anne's, all you think about are those buttery, perfectly baked bites of deliciousness. I want one right now.

She was just missing a few key secret ingredients. Just a few new ingredients changed the whole recipe, and made the difference! Her company is now worth millions and millions of dollars, is found in forty-four states, and over twenty-two countries! And to think she almost gave up on the pretzels!

You are my 'little pretzel'. If you are feeling like you are a product that should be 'taken off the menu' hang in there. We just need to discover your secret ingredients! It's that simple. By the way, if after reading this book, you happen to change your net worth to the millions category, I would like to request a 10% commission. I'm not kidding. 10% straight off the top. And the rights to your first movie. And your first child.

So. You want to discover what your special giftings are. What makes you stand out from the crowd. What sets you apart. What your secret-no-one-else-has-it ingredient is. This, you're going to enjoy. Hopefully. Of course, I'm one of those odd creatures that always enjoys doing the 'personality tests'. I suppose that is my personality category! 'Hello, I'm a melancholy', 'Hello, I'm a passive-aggressive'...."HELLO, My name is Kirsten, and I'm an Enjoying Personality Test Taker. Nice to meet you".

This won't hurt you one bit. I promise. No list of 1000 questions. I'll even be super nice. If you don't want to be involved in this activity, you can skip right over this whole section. You will hurt my feelings, and possibly not discover a hidden talent that could make you famous one day, but I want to give you that option. I'm setting you free. If you love someone, set them free. If they come back they're yours; if they don't they never were. (I think I wrote that quote in letters to a few boyfriends in the 1980's).

So I will begin by asking you a few simple questions. Do you have your #2 pencil sharpened and ready? You don't? That's OK, remember, I told you this would be pain-free. No pencils required for Mrs. Hart's class. I'm the cool teacher.

What do you love to do? It sounds so simple, doesn't it. Believe it or not, some people have never taken the time to sit down and ponder what they love to do. What you love to do usually helps define your skills and passion. Most of us wouldn't list things that we're bad at doing in our list of 'things we love to do'. Usually the things you love to do, you're naturally good at. I don't love to do math because I'm horrible at it. I love to sing. I love to bake. I love to decorate my house. These are activities that I love to doing, and that other people have confirmed 'you're pretty good at this'.

Many of us have grown up in church environments where we are discouraged from putting ourselves in the fore-front. It's vain to talk about ourselves and what we may be good or talented at. Isn't that sad? Here God poured all of these unique batches of giftedness into every individual, and church leadership and members want to quiet us. Be humble. Shh. Pride cometh before the fall. I've heard that saying quoted as pure scripture. Wrong! That's not even found in the Bible! The verse in reference is actually, Proverbs 16:18, 'Pride goeth before destruction, and an haughty spirit before a fall.' Which, isn't the most encouraging verse ever found anyways. That thought has abused so many people in church to almost suffocate their gifts and passions.

This is a new day! I am here to announce that it is not prideful to know your gifts and passions. It's not wrong to talk to others about what you're good at. Now if you start getting too big for your britches, and thinking that you're better than everybody else, we may need to sit and have a chat.

I've met some sweet, sweet people in churches, and have asked them what they're good at. "Well, nothing, really" is a response I have too often heard. So sad. People have gone their whole lives thinking there's nothing that they're particularly good at. Ask the same question, "What do you love to do", and you get a whole different response.

My grandfather used to have a huge garden in his side yard in Erie, Pennsylvania. Not a fancy man, my Grandpa Caldwell. He was a welding specialist at a factory there, yet he also produced some of the best corn and tomatoes you could ever put inside your mouth. I'm sure if you were to ask him what he was good at, he would have replied, 'Oh, nothing in particular', yet he was one of the best garden farmers ever. I know he enjoyed working in his garden, but yet wouldn't particularly say that he was good at it. He could have easily sold his produce at farmers markets, and won blue ribbons. He indeed was good at what he loved doing.

I know I was joking earlier about needing a sharpened #2 pencil. Well, if you have the time, I would love for you to write down a list. You won't be graded on this, and you can use a pencil or a pen. Whatever your heart desires to write with.

Next, make a list. This list should include all the things you're good at. This list can be as simple or complex as you wish. Are you good at cleaning windows? Write it down. Are you good at photography? Write it down. Do you grow the best zucchini this side of the Mississippi River? Write it down. If you're worried about someone else in your household seeing this list, and them getting the idea that you're becoming a Diva or 'Divo', then hide the list. They can make up their own list if they so choose to read this book. (Now who's talking like a Diva???)

I'll be nice and give you a few starting ideas. You may have similar interests to this list, or the things listed may be polar opposites of what you feel your gifts are. Either way, it's a good start to you creating your own list.

- Building things
- Fixing things
- Investigating things
- Making connections
- Building relationships
- Creating dialogue
- Healing wounds
- Adding humor
- Persuading people
- Organizing things

- Selling things
- Doing the numbers
- Resolving disputes
- Instructing others
- Optimizing things
- Making deals
- Starting things
- Designing things
- Researching things
- Seeing the big picture
- Writing things
- Solving problems

Get carried away. Have a blast. You're not being prideful, you're recognizing the gifts God has put into you. This is healthy, trust me. Much healthier than the candy corn I have been nibbling on while writing this chapter.

Now take that #2 pencil and sharpen it again. I know. I lied. I said you weren't going to have to use a pencil. Will you forgive me? Blame it on the nature of the beast. The beast of finding your inner gifts. But that would be a nice beast wouldn't it. Again, if you want to skip this exercise, feel free. But I think you may enjoy it.

Here's what I want you to do. Answer by writing the very first thing that comes to mind with the following questions. Don't take a lot of time thinking about each item. The quicker you answer, the more pure the answer. OK, here you go:

•As a child, what did you love to do? Write? Read? Sports? Working on models? Playing with a chemistry set? Spending time outdoors? Pretending to be a solider or a spy? Baking? Sewing?

•During school group projects, what job did other students assign to you, or did you volunteer for?

•What aspects of your current job do you love, which do you loathe?

•What kinds of projects and jobs at work and at home do you get excited about? What kinds do you dread?

•Have you ever talked to a friend about a topic, a dream, or an aspiration and everything just clicked inside of you, and you felt a surge of excitement throughout your body?

•What things do you see other people doing that make you ache with jealousy because you wish you were doing them?

•What issues get you really fired up?

•Have you ever talked to a friend about a topic, a dream, or an aspiration and everything just clicked inside of you, and you felt a surge of excitement throughout your body?

•What things do you see other people doing that make you (in a good way?) envious because you wish you were doing them?

•What were you doing the last time you totally lost track of time?

Are all these questions overwhelming you a bit? I totally understand. Take a little break. Perhaps you need to go get yourself a glass of chocolate milk, or make yourself a s'more. Those two items usually comfort and relax me.

Are you done with your little break? Time to dig in just a little more. I promise the rest of the chapters will feel like a cake walk after this one!

Now, this may take some of you WAY out of your comfort zone, but trust me, it's all worth it. Live a little. Go a little farther out on the branch. Trust me for a bit, will you? The end result will be worth it all.

Here's what you can do. Brace yourself. Here we go. Ask some of your friends what they think you're good at. GASP! See, now, this would be as natural as breathing to me. Of course, I'd try to make it rather humorous, but this activity lines right up with my taking those Personality Tests. I wasn't a shy one in school. Can you tell?

Now get ready to be surprised and (hopefully blessed). Unless they're all horrible to you and say that you're not good at anything. If that is the case you need to get new friends. I'll be your friend. Don't worry. I know I could find things you're good at!

Does it freak you out to ask someone what they think you are good at? Try not to think about it too long and hard. Friends sometimes can see things about us that we can't see ourselves. I'll bet you'll be shocked at what people will tell you. 'Me?' 'You think I'm good at that?' I'm smiling right now thinking about how (hopefully great) this activity will work out for you.

So take your multiple paged list of what you're good at. Look at it long and hard. Give yourself a big smile. Give yourself a hug. You are so talented. God has given you so many giftings. See? Slap yourself on the back. 'Well look at me, I do have things I'm good at.' Now, you don't have to go around the house telling your whole family that you just found out you are indeed God's gift to the world. A little humility is a nice thing.

Congratulations. Now I want you to work on another list. Don't worry, I'm not requiring you to come up with all these lists in the same day. If you're an overachiever, go for it. If you struggled just to come up with a few items for the last list, take a breather. No pressure. Just somewhere down the road take out another piece of paper and jot down these thoughts.

What excites you?

That's your question. This time don't think long and hard. Just start freely writing what excites you in life. What do you love. What are you passionate about? What gets your heart racing?

What excites you could be a hobby, a side job, something you do as a volunteer, parent, or spouse. It could be something you haven't done in a long time. On your marks, get set, GO!

Are you exhausted? I know. This is a lot of work. I think you'll enjoy the end result. You might even stir up some life passions that you have forgotten about. 'Oh, I completely forgot that I used to enjoy that. That was a big part of who I was. I haven't done that in years. Why?' Self-re-discovery can be a great thing. It's energizing.

FINAL LIST details: (I hope this one is fun for you, too). Now write down what you have secretly dreamed of doing. Have fun with this. This is your time to go crazy, my friends. Again, this is your list. Brainstorm. If you want to share this list with your family and loved ones, go for it. If not, keep it for yourself. Whatever floats your boat.

Have you wanted to be a novelist, an artist, a designer, an architect, a doctor, an entrepreneur, or programmer? But some fear, some self-doubt, has held you back. Maybe there are several careers or goals you have dreamed about. Add them to the list, no matter how unrealistic you may think they are.

Now take a Caribbean cruise and enjoy reading all of your lists. Go ahead. You'll enjoy it. You deserve it. Tell your spouse I told you so.

When you're back from the cruise, take your lists

out again. Granted, you may have to wipe all the sand off the papers, but it'll be worth it.

Now re-glance over your lists. Do you see any common threads? Do you see any items that appear on all the lists? Is there something on the lists that has re-inspired you? Didn't realize that you were good at something that a friend saw in you? Could that untapped gift work in unison with that dream career you have always thought about? 'Gosh, Joe said that I was great at fixing computers. I never thought I was that good at it? Perhaps I could repair computers as I side job while I'm going back to school for my computer degree'.

Reinvention isn't necessarily just about finding a *new* career, job, talent, or gifting. It's also about harvesting what God has already placed inside of you. Perhaps those dreams, desires, and talents have been in hiding for a while. Rediscovering who God naturally intended for you to be is part of the reinvention process. And you are well on your way!

A whole new world of possibilities awaits you. Perhaps you have realized new dreams. God is the giver of dreams, and I promise you, he's not done creating, or giving dreams. Perhaps he's waiting to give you a brand new passion that will excite you beyond what you thought possible for your life.

The best, my friends, is still to come! If you haven't realized your secret ingredient yet, keep searching. It's bound to be somewhere in the cupboard of your heart. See it? Maybe you have to reach way in the back, but it'll be worth it. Once you add that secret ingredient to your life, there's no stopping you. Get ready to take off!

NEGATIVE
NELLIE AND NED

I so don't want to give anyone named Nellie or Ned a bad rap. Please, once again, forgive me if you happen to have one of these names, and you're greatly offended. You have to admit, though, that the word negative does really go easily with the names Nellie and Ned. It kind of flows.

I don't want to take forever on this chapter. Although it is an important one. The purpose of writing this chapter? *Stay away from negative people.* I know you're thinking, 'Easier said than done'. Trust me, I understand.

I'm not old. Well, not really old. I am currently forty-eight years old. I love my age. I am no longer referred to as 'such a child' and yet no one is signing me up for the local nursing home. This is a great age. I have lived enough life that people will fairly respect my opinion now, yet young enough to still enjoy platform shoes.

One thing I have learned in my forty-eight years of living? The kinds of people I like to surround myself with. I like funny people. I like intelligent (but not too intelligent) people. You know what I mean. Some really smart people can only talk about things like Pythagorean theorems and the theory of relativity. My brain doesn't function in theorems. I function in the latest episodes of certain reality TV programs, and great new recipes I found online. Mine is a simpler existence.

I like people that share common interests. I like people that can step up and do what it takes in a situation, and not complain. I like encouraging people. I like positive people. I like people that make me laugh, and look on the bright side of life.

We recently had dinner with some friends in Orlando when we were down there. (You'll read about my Space Mountain experience later on in the book). I had met this couple before, but had never shared a meal together, or got beyond the 'nice to meet you's'. Dave knew them well, but it had been twenty-four years since he had been around them.

We met for dinner at 6:30. We closed the place down at 11, when the waiters started hauling out the vacuum cleaners. There hadn't been one single awkward pause. No "I think I may run to the restroom because this is completely boring me and I need a break" incident. We had non-stop wonderful stimulating conversation, and in fact continued chatting once we were standing outside of the restaurant.

That kind of scenario is *gold* to me. It doesn't happen all the time, and when it does, you know you have connected in a way with someone that is so precious and rare. Those are the friendships that I want to foster.

I don't want you to think that I will only associate with those who share similar interests. Believe you me, as a Worship Pastor's wife, I have learned that it is wise (and a blessing) to spend time with all kinds of people. And I have. But in all the years of meeting and greeting and eating, I have come to realize the kind of person that is stimulating and uplifting to be around. Those are the people I choose to be around when I have a choice.

Let's say you're a fireman. Now, you can go out to eat with all sorts of people, but when you have the opportunity to be with a group of other firemen, there is a common bond, and thread that ties you all together. Fellow firemen can relate to you in a way that computer graphic artists never could. You see what I'm saying here, yes?

But there's more. It's vital to who you are, to be surrounded by positive people. Now I'm about to say something rather gutsy. Buckle up. It may be a rough ride. *You need to break off relationships with those that tear you down and discourage you.*

You still with me?

I know I said that I was going to make this chapter short, but whole volumes of books could be written on the topic of breaking off unhealthy relationships. Can you think of someone right now who discourages you and tears down your thoughts and dreams? Have you continued in that relationship because you want to, or because you think it would hurt their feelings to walk away from them?

There are all kinds of reasons why we stay in unhealthy relationships and friendships. But I want to challenge you a bit right now. If you are surrounded by dream and vision stealers, you will never fully evolve into who you were designed and created to be. You will never be wholly you if you listen to all the negative voices.

The tough part? Some of these negatively voiced people are your own family members. You're stuck with them, right? Perhaps you can't decline the acceptance to the annual Thanksgiving Day festivities, but you can filter the time spent talking directly with them. You can filter how much time is spent in their presence. You can filter how many times you hear them on the phone cutting your ideas down. You can filter their ramblings. Have you heard of Caller I.D.? It's genius. Now I'm not promoting rudeness, but I am promoting self-preservation.

If God has called you to a certain purpose in life, and you continue to surround yourself with those who verbally cut you and your calling, you need to make a choice. Choose between God's plan for your life, or to be stuck in a rut with those pulling you down.

I know this is hard stuff. I know it's not easy. But I want you to live whole. Whole in your ultimate calling and purpose. Fulfilled, not frustrated. Inspired, not irritated.

If you feel that indeed there are some people that you need to start filtering out their involvement in your life, hold fast. First Peter 4:4-5 talks about what happens with old friends, once you have become a Christian, but I believe these verses also apply to letting go of unhealthy friendships. "Of course, your old friends don't understand why you don't join in with the old gang anymore. But you don't have to give an account to them. They're the ones who will be called on the carpet—and before God himself."

Jesus, himself understands letting go of those who do not believe the way you do. He had towns and villages full of people that rejected what he had to say. When Jesus first sent his disciples out on their own to 'drive out evil spirits and to heal every illness and sickness', he gave some specific instructions and great wisdom concerning the people they were to stay with.

"When you enter a town or village, look for someone who is willing to welcome you. Stay at that person's house until you leave. As you enter the home, greet those who live there. If that home welcomes you, give it your blessing of peace. If it does not, don't bless it. Some people may not welcome you or listen to your words. If they don't, shake the dust off your feet when you leave that home or town." Matthew 10: 11-14.

In Biblical times, when leaving Gentile cities, pious Jews often shook the dust from their feet to show their separation from Gentile practices. If the disciples shook the dust of a Jewish town from their feet, it would show their separation from Jews who rejected their Messiah. The gesture was to show the people that they were making a wrong choice. The opportunity to choose Christ might not present itself again.

Such great instruction. We need to take those words into our own lives, as we go about trying to make a difference in our world. If you're not accepted or welcome, shake the unwelcome dust off your feet, and move on. Move on to other relationships that are positive and welcoming. Move on to relationships that speak words of life, not discouragement.

Can I get an A-MEN out there?

You may not be able to jump head in on the whole distancing yourself from unhealthy relationships, but find a place to start. Start with baby steps if you need to. If every time you talk to a particular friend, you find yourself discouraged afterward, start limiting those calls. It's OK to monitor your calls. Trust me. There's no law that states you have to talk to everyone that calls you. Be selective. Be wise. Guard your heart and your dreams.

It's not easy. I know. Neither is losing weight, but I tell you, once you have dropped even ten pounds, you don't ever want to be walking around with that extra weight again. You never knew you could feel so good. It's the same with unhealthy relationships.

Another Bible verse: I John 2:19 is in reference to antichrists who tried to deceive people. I, personally feel it also refers to those who come against us, and try to harm us. "They left us, but they were never really with us. If they had been, they would have stuck it out with us, loyal to the end. In leaving, they showed their true colors, showed they never did belong."

There are people in the world who are dream and vision stealers. They want to suck the very life out of you. They want to discourage you. They feel bad about themselves, so in order to make themselves look and feel better, they drag you down to their level. Be strong. Resist. Rise above.

Instead of being friends with Negative Nellie and Ned, try meeting some new folks in the neighborhood, Positive Patty and Pete. Oh, and that new family that just moved in down the block, Encouraging Edith and Eddie. I hear Edith makes the best double chocolate brownies ever!

Straight To The
Principal's Office

Now first off, I need to address something in the title of this chapter. I, like so many other wide-eyed innocents in elementary school learned how to spell principal with a cutesy little trick. Teachers taught their students to spell principal, as in the head dictator of their school, in such a way as to remember that the 'principal is your *pal*, versus the other spelling, principle (which is something you try to hold true to when in the presence of a princiPAL).

My rebel life started early. In Mrs. Jones' third grade class, my two best friends, Madzy Besselar and Julianne Mulusky, and I thought we would be artistic and creative, and drew wonderful designs all over our spelling books. Now mind you, these weren't the school-owned hardback books that had to survive generations of third grade students. These were the soft-back workbooks that would be ours to keep forever once the last school bell of the year had sounded.

We thought our books looked so much better decorated with hearts and stars. Mrs. Jones didn't. I usually liked her. Mrs. Jones was one of the younger, prettier teachers that year. On this day, however, she had turned into the Wicked Witch of the West (even though we were in East Coast New Jersey).

She, in not a nice manner, told the three of us that we were to take the biggest erasers we could find, and go out in the HALL and erase every bit of our artwork. "Erase it all, until the books look brand new again."

The *hall*??!!! That was the corridor of shame in elementary school! And wasn't it just our good fortune that some of the neighboring classes had to line up to make their way to the lunch room at the very time we were sitting and erasing. The finger pointing and snickering was enough to make us feel like the most wanted criminals in the Wild West. We were bad girls. We had done something shameful. There were fingers pointing at us.

What we were doing was being creative, thank you very much. I haven't been in touch with Madzy and Julianne since junior high, but I can betchya they're creative and artistic women! Mean Mrs. Jones. Wonder what she's up to?

Middle school was my time when I met with the

principal on a regular basis. I honestly think she hated me. Really. I was attending a small Christian school at the time, Mercer Christian Academy, with Satan as the principal. (I didn't just write that did I?) I can't believe I forgot the name of the principal. Gosh, what was it? See, she was so mean that my self-conscious has purposefully blocked her name from my memory. Thank you self-conscious! You got my back!

I was friends with the principal's daughter, Debbie. That's funny, I can remember her daughter's first name, but not the last. AHHH! It just came to me! Mrs. MILLER! Do you know her? Not a nice woman.

So I was friends with her daughter, but we were in a *trio* with Dianne. There were the three of us: Dianne, Debbie, and Kirsten. Now, women, you know what a threesome of middle school girls is don't you? TROUBLE with a capital T. Seriously. Perhaps four days out of the month, we were a happy trio of best friends. The other twenty-some days one of us was 'out'. Now raise your hand if you remember the whole 'out' thing. (Sorry guys reading this book, you'll just have to bear with me through this girl stuff. Take it as a freebie lesson in middle school female life.)

So, one friend may say something even a teeny weenie bit catty about one of the trio, and if we were in the mood, the one who said the comment would be 'out' until further notice. You were out of being 'in' the trio of friends. And, yes, periodically, even I was out sometimes. It's life in middle school. It's probably the basis for Darwin's Theory of Evolution. Survival of the fittest. (Well, actually Herbert Spencer originated that phrase, but Darwin used it later on). Needless to say, middle school was tough. Mrs. Miller was tougher.

It seemed as if every time that Debbie was 'out' I was 'in'. In the principal's office, that is. I think Debbie was narking to her mother. I also believe that Debbie got her revenge on the two who were keeping her 'out' by telling her mom things we did that would be possible reasons to visit the principal's office. Mrs. Miller was Debbie's personal mafia. 'You mess with my family, I mess with you...'

One of the times I was in Mrs. Miller's office, I'll will admit, was justified. Mrs. Brown was my seventh grade teacher at Mercer Christian Academy. In fact, the school was so small that she was the only seventh grade teacher. On most days, she was nice. Not the coolest teacher in the world, but nice. One afternoon she was in a rather crotchety mood. Heck, I probably would have been, too, if I were stuck in a room with 7th graders day in and day out.

Well, I was not so thrilled to be sitting under the teacher-ship of Mrs. Brown that day. So, I thought it would be funny to randomly place a few thumbtacks on her desk chair. A few of the other students thought it would be funny, too, and dared and egged me on. I took the bait.

We had to wait until the math work on the board was complete, but then it happened. Mrs. Brown started walking towards her chair. When she pulled it out, I caught my breath. She sat down, and then immediately popped back up. I couldn't help it. It made me laugh.

"Who did this??!" she yelled. Every finger pointed in my direction. Busted. Back down to Mrs. Miller's office. Oh, joy.

Looking back now, I seriously can't believe I did that. Hey KIDS, don't listen to peer pressure! You'll end up in the principal's office, if not worse! Take this as a lesson from Mrs. Hart. Is it wrong to admit that the look on Mrs. Brown's face when she popped up was rather hilarious? It is wrong, isn't it.

The majority of the times that I got in trouble, I was getting in trouble for (hold your surprise here) TALKING TOO MUCH. Yeh, big shocker, huh. I, Kirsten Hart, talked too much. (I think I may have written something like that on the chalkboard a few times). But who's laughing now? I make a LIVING by talking! Lookie there! What I used to get in trouble for, is now how I make my living. I'm smiling as I'm writing this. "So there, Mrs. Miller."

Your talents, unrefined are usually what you got in trouble for in school. Refine those talents, and you'll find your great strength!

See, there's hope for those little ones that visit the principal's office! We're just souls expressing our gifts that don't necessarily fit into the regimen and restrictions of a school building. We talkers were just communicators in need of the proper outlet. Once I discovered that I loved to speak before audiences, it's as if the 3rd grade girl in me came alive. No one told me to 'shush', and yet people actually listened to what I had to say!

I'm not alone, remember those class clowns that you used to laugh at in school? Lots of them are making the big bucks on stages before thousands, sharing their humor. Sent out to get on their CUSTOM COACH BUS instead of in the HALL!

You have seriously lived either under a rock, or in an Amish community if you have not heard of actor and comedian Jim Carrey. He has made umpteen movies, and is a bona fide Hollywood star. If probably wouldn't surprise you to find out that he was actually a class clown in school.

"Carrey has always been the class clown. His elementary school teacher, instead of punishing him for being rowdy and disruptive, made a deal. If Carrey would sit quietly during class without bugging his classmates, in exchange he would get a bit of time set aside at the end of every day to put on an act for them. It was in these early "performances" that he mastered his impressions and battled his self-proclaimed introversion and shyness." --An internet article written on Jim Carrey's life

See! Great, creative minds just need some guidance. I love that Jim's teacher gave him the reward of coming to the front of the class, and doing his impressions. I have read that during those post-class routines is where he created some of his well-known impressions that made him so famous. There's hope!

78

JustDisney.com shared an article about our beloved Walt Disney. "After Walt's birth, the Disney family moved to Marceline, Missouri. Walt lived out most of his childhood here. Walt had a very early interest in drawing, and art. When he was seven years old, he sold small sketches, and drawings to nearby neighbors. Instead of doing his school work Walt doodled pictures of animals, and nature.

His knack for creating enduring art forms took shape when he talked his sister, Ruth, into helping him paint the side of the family's house with tar."

No one would argue that Walt Disney wasn't one of the greatest creative minds and Imagineers of the twentieth century. Yet, even he 'doodled' instead of doing homework! Just think what I could have done with myself if Mrs. Jones hadn't stifled my creativity back in the 3rd grade!

Don't miss one of the best parts of Walt's childhood story. He and his sister painted the side of their HOUSE with TAR!!! I love it! Now there's a creative genius as a child. Am I giving some of you parents hope for your children? Of course children need direction, but some of their greatest untapped talents and giftings appear in rather odd ways sometimes when they are young.

You know those boys that used to create guns out of paperclips and endless rubber bands? Betchya they're engineers now! Those boys that used to non-stop build tinker toy bridges and fortresses. They've probably built skyscrapers!

As parents, learn to see what gifts your children have through how they enjoy spending their time. How they spend their time and what they get in trouble for. Do you have an arguer? Arguing children can grow up to be excellent lawyers!

What did you like to do as a child that sometimes got you in trouble? Perhaps that was your calling in an unrefined state.

There's always a silver lining. Sometimes you just have to search for it. Think twice before disciplining your child for doodling instead of doing homework. Take a look at those drawings. You may have a future Walt Disney on your hands.

Isn't God good? He can take what are seemingly our downfalls character-wise, and reinvent them into our strengths!

Now if your child happens to paint tar all over your house, you may have to take lots of deep breaths, and dig down to China to find that silver lining!

No Thanks, But Thank You Though

Our first year of marriage found us in Nashville, Tennessee. We had dated in Orlando, but moved to Nashville after we had our wedding in Denver. It's complicated. We'll have lunch sometime, and I can map out the time-line for you.

It was an exciting time in our life. We loaded up the smallest U-Haul you could rent, filled it with a dresser Dave had bought at a garage sale for $15, a few pots and pans, my cello, and our three suitcases. The U-Haul was attached to the back of Dave's white Chevy Chevette, and we headed up north. We were on a newlywed adventure.

We were Bally's Health Club members at the time, so we searched for an apartment near the only Bally's in town. Our new residence was a small one-bedroom apartment on Paragon Mill Road, just off of Harding Place and I-24. Know the area? It was near the old Harding Mall on Nolensville Road. I've heard the mall was demolished, and there's now a Super Walmart sitting in its place. I also have read that the area isn't what it used to be. Even twenty-five years ago it wasn't much. But it didn't matter to us. We were in love.

We chose an apartment in the older building of the complex, because the apartment was more spacious than the newer ones. Funny to think of now. It was tiny, but we made it homey. What were our end tables made out of you ask? Why they were fashioned from our moving boxes covered with table cloths from Kmart. Burgundy colored table cloths. And our dining table you wonder? Why, that was a fancy square card table complete with folding captain's chairs.

We went all out in the master bedroom, though. We found a king size box mattress and two twin mattresses to complete the set. You just had to be careful not to sleep on the crack between the two twin mattresses. You couldn't walk upright in the morning if you did. I still can't believe we hauled those mattresses from the garbage pile at a near-by storage facility. It makes me laugh now. We didn't even think about bed bugs or lice. We sprayed a can of Lysol over the mattresses, sprayed on a can of Woolite rug cleaner, scrubbed it, and hoped for the best. Again, it was OK, because we were in love.

Although small and sparse, our first little nest was cozy and comfy. A lot of love and laughter filled those walls. Two months after we moved in we bought a puppy, Cuddles. Our young newly formed family was complete.

Dave had some great connections in Nashville, and was planning on doing quite a bit of studio singing as his main source of income. I got a steady part-time job as a Fragrance Model for the now deceased Castner-Knott stores. I worked exclusively 'spraying' Liz Claiborne fragrances. I had bottles and bottles of free fragrance that year. The perks of being a Fragrance Model. Yeah, I had quite the important career. In addition to the hourly income I was making squirting people with perfume, I also taught modeling classes at the Nashville Barbizon School of Modeling. I was climbing up the corporate level at rocket speed.

We did some sessions too, but work wasn't as steady as we had hoped. So Dave started looking for a part-time church position.

He interviewed, and got a Minister of Music position at Leeville Baptist Church right near Mt. Juliet, Tennessee. It was an old-fashioned all-wood church building. Wood pews, squeaky wood floors, wooden beams, and a wooden choir loft. You couldn't walk or sit anywhere in that sanctuary without it creaking. You couldn't adjust the way you were sitting during the sermon without the whole church hearing 'cr-e-e-e-e-k'. The place could probably seat 100 people comfortably, and on Sundays the pews were filled with some of the sweetest people we had ever met.

Dave took the position the beginning of November that year. Being the musical pro that he is, he scrambled to put together a nice Christmas program for the choir to perform, and the congregation to enjoy. The ink on Dave's contract wasn't even dry when I was approached by the Children's Choir Committee.

"We would love for you to take the children's Christmas musical over, since you're so good at music" were the words coming at my direction. "We think you'd be so good with the kids, and we could really use your help."

You know the kind of girls, when you were growing up, who always were holding someone's babies, worked in the church nursery, and babysat every child in the neighborhood? It wasn't me. Don't get me wrong, I liked kids, but I wasn't a kid fanatic like some other girls were. Kids were cute. They made me laugh. I just wasn't dying to work in a daycare, or teach the three and four year-old Sunday school class.

Now, hold your judgments and predictions of my mothering abilities. When I had my own two boys, there was nothing better than being with my babies at every stage of their growing up. The mothering gene kicked in. It's all good.

Now to jump back to my 1990 scenario. Did I want to take over the Children's Christmas Musical? Nope. No, thank you. I was a busy fragrance model (four hours a day, thank you very much) plus my modeling class students. My workload was full. I was a newlywed. I had enough on my plate. Plus, I wanted to make homemade heart-shaped Christmas tree ornaments for our very first Christmas tree that year. Could a woman be any busier? (Tongue very much in cheek).

So my heart and head said no, but out of my mouth came the word, "yes". I instantly was in charge of the whole children's musical. And I found out that rehearsals were on Sunday nights plus additional Saturday rehearsals. Ugh.

Now hold your mean comments and thoughts. There is a point to all of this. The point won't be what a horrible person I am, though. I'll attempt to redeem myself.

I directed all the rehearsals. We had the musical performance. It went great. The kids did great. They sounded great. People were happy. They thanked me profusely. They handed me flowers at the end of the performance. All hunky-dory.

Have I, over the other twenty-five years of marriage accepted the role of helping out in an area where I really don't want to help? Yes. Did those scenarios turn out horrendously horrible? No. Did I enjoy my time helping out with those requests? Honestly? Not really.

Here's the deal. Yes, I realize that in life, sometimes we need to step up and do things that help others, and put us out of our complete comfort zone. Yes, I understand that life isn't always about getting our way, and being happy 100% of the time. Yes, I believe that it is important to help in the church. But we need to work within our giftings.

This is the important factor. I have seen many people volunteer and help out in departments that aren't where they belong. Do they help? Yes? Do they fill a need? Yes. But, if they're not serving using their specific gifts, they're serving out of duty rather than passion. Keep with me here.

Here's an example. Now I'm baring my soul. When my babies were young, the church we were serving in had a rule. If you had children in the nursery, you yourself had to work one Sunday a month in the nursery yourself, taking care of your baby, plus everyone else's child.

I am a proponent of hiring nursery workers, by the way. The last thing I wanted to do after being with my two baby boys all week was to get all dressed up, put make-up on, and come to church to watch my boys and a nursery full of other babies. There was only one service, so all you got to do that Sunday was work in the nursery. It would have been so much easier to just stay at home in my pajamas. I know there have to be at least a few of you reading this that have walked in my exact shoes.

So, here I was, a tired mom of two babies under 3 getting dressed up to change diapers all morning. Again, was I grateful for the other three Sundays that other moms changed my babies diapers? You bet. Extremely grateful.

I fed the babies, I changed a few diapers, I even sat on the floor while everyone crawled around, but I know I didn't give my whole heart to those babies on Sunday mornings. Some of the moms in there did. They were in the center of their calling and gifting with those babies. They loved taking care of the children. That's where their ministry calling was. They loved those Sunday mornings. I trudged through them. Some of those babies that I was responsible for even went back to their parents without having their diaper freshly changed. My bad. Please don't throw me by the wayside quite yet.

Now, with all this talk of needing to volunteer and help out aside, which mom would you rather have taking care of your babies in the nursery? The mothers who lived for their Sunday morning time in the nursery, or me?

The other mothers, right! Why? Because the other mothers had a passion for children.

Think of those that have been asked to help out in children's church because there wasn't anyone else, but they don't really like children. (Believe me, this happens all the time). You don't want someone that can't stand toddlers teaching your three year-old every Sunday morning, do you? I hope not. People are wrangled into ministry positions where they never should be.

Are you still my friend? Do you think I'm a horrible volunteer?

Now, would you allow me to show you my good

side? Place me in my calling, and I thrive. Speak to the women of the church? 100% yes vote. Sing in choir? 100% yes vote. Sing on the Praise Team? 100% yes vote. Work on a solo for Sunday morning? 100% yes vote. Clean toilets and cook for someone that is needy? 100% yes vote. Help serve and cook in the kitchen? 100% yes vote.

Those are volunteer positions that fit my calling, passion, and gifting. It makes all the difference. If everyone in the church were placed into volunteer positions that fit their calling, the church would run so smooth, and ministries wouldn't have to beg for people to help out where they shouldn't be helping.

I have learned a valuable word. It's just a small word, but as I got older and wiser, I added it to my vocabulary. The word is: no. Now, you have to say it nicely, but it is a viable word to speak in church. I have learned, over the years, that in certain circumstances it is OK to tell someone 'no'. I'm not saying no to helping out because I am being selfish, or only want the most noticeable and 'glorified' spots in church. I am saying 'no', because deep down, I am not the person to best fill that role.

Example: I was asked to head up a Children's Summer Music Camp for a whole week, with the week concluding with a full-blown kid's musical. I know myself. I would have dreaded every rehearsal. So I said 'no'. Gasp! What I did volunteer for? Being the snack lady! And I loved it! I enjoyed planning different creative snacks and drinks for the whole week. The kids had great snacks because I used what I was gifted at in a service ministry role.

Having the guts to say no to leading the camp opened the door for someone else to step in to that leadership position. Guess what? She loved directing the kids, and she put on one fantastic production! Way better than I could or would have done. In my saying "no", I opened the door for someone better for the kids.

"But I have to say yes."

If you feel down deep that you have to, then by all means do it. I just want to encourage you to be honest with yourself, and be able to identify what you do best, and to be able to enjoy what you do. I am a firm believer that everyone is happier, and benefits from people properly placed in their serving roles.

I have been pressured that 'no one else can take your place'. Believe-it-or-not, there usually is someone else that can fill my shoes. Rather easily, actually. If you reluctantly keep accepting positions that you later regret, just think of those better suited people who could have stepped up to take that role if you had said "No, thank you."

I know this is a different viewpoint than you will hear in most churches, but this is coming from my heart to yours. My parents were Ministers of Music, and I married a Worship Pastor. I literally have spent my whole life in a church leadership family. I have seen it all. We'll go get smoothies someday, and I'll tell you some stories! And do I have stories!

This chapter is written out of love. This chapter is to encourage you to walk in the unique special path God has created for you. When you walk and serve him using the gifts he specifically placed in you, you will walk as a fulfilled and happy person. You will enjoy serving and volunteering, and you will say "yes" to requests that suit you. You won't have to dread saying "No thanks, but thank you though", and feel guilty every time you see that person who asked you to help out. As the owner of the Men's Warehouse says in his commercials, "I guarantee it."

*One final thought: I don't believe that God will reinvent you for a career/job/calling that isn't suited for what he already placed inside of you. I am horrible at math. Therefore I don't believe God is going to reinvent me into a Trigonometry teacher. So take a deep breath. God has wonderful and exciting plans for your future.

Apple Orchard Lane

I must have been three or four when we went there. We were living in upstate New York. Plattsburgh, New York. On Saturdays we would drive to the apple orchard. I don't have full recall of the orchard, just snapshots of memories. I do remember sipping free samples of apple cider, buying a crate of apples and a gallon of apple cider whenever we visited. If my memory serves me correctly, the orchard itself was located on Apple Orchard Lane. That name made it through all the other memories over the forty years after my orchard visiting days. To this day, I love that name.

Something about the name Apple Orchard Lane stirs feelings of warmth, down-home-ness, and quaintness. All from that little apple orchard! I bet they never realized the impact they were having on that little strawberry blonde toddler that visited them on Saturdays in the Fall!

Thanks to Apple Orchard Lane, I now have sort of a mild obsession with comforting street names. It's not really an obsession, but I can't come up with a better name. OK, I have a 'thing' for street names. Does that make any more sense?

When we lived in Tulsa, Oklahoma, we lived on East 75th Court. Now, while I enjoy the title 'court', nothing with the East 75th made our address feel cozy. I like cozy street names.

Our home in Colorado Springs was located on Hartman Drive. We built that house new, and had the choice of building it on either Poudre or Hartman. Come on, that was a no brainer! When we introduced ourselves to neighbors, we would say, "We're the Harts on Hartman". Now, isn't that just the cutest thing you have ever heard? Perfect street name for our family of three men and a girl.

Houston had some great street names. When we lived there for three years, our home address was 13123 Finch Brook Drive. Doesn't that just make you smile? A sweet little finch fluttering over a crystal clear flowing brook. Ahhh. What a pretty visual. See, now you're starting to understand my 'thing' with street names, right?

Our last house was 200 Brown Street. Now, while that name may not evoke emotions of coziness, it did quaintly remind me of an address that Sesame Street characters might live on.

I saw a house listed for sale the other day on a realtor website, and the house was on Peach Orchard Lane. So very close to my perfect Apple Orchard! Unfortunately, the house was in dire need of repair for the asking price, but honestly, I think I could have lived out the rest of my days in perfect bliss if given the opportunity own a home on Peach Orchard Lane.

Throughout my years, I have always dreamed of some kind of business that I could name 'Apple Orchard Lane'. It's still my favorite road name. We were looking at an adorable completely remodeled farm house near our hometown. It was an 1890's farmstead that had been taken down to the studs and completely rebuilt. I loved it. The only thing I didn't love was its resale value. The house directly across the street had twenty rusted cars in the front yard and about fifteen dogs running unchained.

If we had bought the farmhouse, I had plans to have a sign made with the name Apple Orchard Lane on it, and I would have placed that sign at the beginning of our driveway. Of course, staying true to the name, I had also envisioned planting apple trees to line the driveway all the way up to the house.

My mind didn't stop with the sign. I had been given a new vision. A new company name. This new name could be my publishing company name for the children's books that have been floating around in my head for the past ten years. This new series of books would be from the company 'The Little White Farm House'. Complete name? 'The Little White Farm House

On Apple Orchard Lane'. Now, doesn't that just evoke sweet fuzzy feelings? My thoughts exactly.

Oh, and those Meal Candles I created? They would have been the Meal Candle *division* of Apple Orchard Lane Candles!

One of these days I'm going to brand my Apple Orchard Lane into something. You just wait and see. I've got a DREAM!

Do you have a dream you've always thought about? Even just a name for your future company? Never stop brainstorming about what you can do. The possibilities are endless. Everything hasn't been created yet. The next great thing that everyone has to have and can't live without is just around the corner! Why couldn't I have thought of wheels on suitcases?! Brilliant!

Perhaps you've had ideas rolling around in your mind for years. Are you one that likes to 'tinker'? Have you come up with a solution to a problem that people need? That's the key! What problem do common everyday people have that needs to be solved? Solve that problem, and you've got it made. Let me once again restate that a 10% royalty fee goes along with any idea you may come up with as a result of reading this book. Now, 10% isn't much to require, is it?

My husband, Dave, reminds me of his invention every time we travel—which is quite frequently. Every time we're in an airport he explains why he needs to flesh out his invention. Years ago he even wrote down his invention, and sent his idea to himself. He said that if he kept the envelope sealed, it would prove that he had copyrighted his idea. I think he still may have that unopened envelope somewhere in our storage boxes. Now after I tell you what his idea is, you can't go inventing it yourself. We have the copyright envelope to prove it was his idea. Remember that.

So this great idea? Dave came up with his idea when he had continuous flight delays, and he was stuck sleeping in an uncomfortable airport seat for hours. Metal arm rests restricted his ability to lie down and actually get comfortable. That's when his copyrighted idea came into being. "Airports need to have reclining Lazy Boy type chairs that have a built in alarm clock, a mini TV, and comes with a fresh pillow and blanket. Oh, and a compartment for your carry-on case, purse, wallet, etc." We have yet to see those available to the general public.

Would you pay a few dollars to enjoy chairs like that? Dave sure would. He thinks lots of people would pay good money for that kind of comfort.

A few months ago we were with Dave's family in San Diego. I'm not sure how we got on the topic, but we were all sitting talking about money-making ideas that we had. Dave was busy chatting with his step dad, so he didn't hear his sister Debi's idea. "I have a great idea. It's for airports. They need to have Lazy Boy chairs with little TV's so that you could relax or sleep during long layovers." The exact words from her mouth. Houston, we have a problem. Now two siblings had the same idea. Déjà vu. Good thing my

Dave had sent that sealed envelope to himself over twenty years ago!

I laughed, and told Debi that I thought that idea was actually Dave's idea, and that I had been hearing Dave talk about that potential money maker for years. "Oh, I don't think so," was her response. Dave was brought into the discussion. Then the cutest sibling debate about who originated the airport Lazy Boy idea ensued. "That's been my idea for as long as I can remember"--Debi. "You're wrong, that's my idea"-- Dave. They're cute, those two.

What's your great idea? You have one, right? That 'if I had a way of making it' idea? That 'perhaps one day I'll work on that' idea. Do you have an invention worth copyrighting?

We were designed as creators. That genetic code is written deep within our human design. Genesis 1:27 states that God created humans in his own image. We were made to resemble God's nature. Well, what is his nature? He is many things, but he is ultimately a creator.

Think about it. The first images we have about God in the Bible are of him creating the world. Creating every plant and living creature, then topping it off with the creation of us! His creating nature is without end. It has never stopped, and is in fact the essence of who he is.

From the beginning of time, he has created. He created the most delicate of flower to the most intricate of minds, the human mind. He creates non-stop. Every second of every minute, hour by hour and day by day he is creating. Every day as new life enters this world, we can physically see the work of his creations. Every flower and even the bugs that are hatched every day are results of this creator who we take after.

My favorite verse out of any song written is found in the hymn The Love Of God. It is one of the most beautiful attempts at explaining the nature of our creator:

Could we with ink the ocean fill,
And were the skies of parchment made,
Were every stalk on earth a quill,
And every man a scribe by trade;
To write the love of God above
Would drain the ocean dry;
Nor could the scroll contain the whole,
Though stretched from sky to sky.

Then the chorus:

Oh, love of God, how rich and pure!
How measureless and strong!
It shall forevermore endure—
The saints' and angels' song.
--Frederick M. Lehman

As beautiful as those words are, they don't even begin to explain how great our God is. Yet he created *us* in his image. How amazing is that? Pretty amazing.

He created us to be creators ourselves. Isn't that exciting?! His very nature of creating is implanted in the depths of our being. So when you or I brainstorm about new inventions or have a desire to create new products, we are tapping into our God-nature. In essence, your DNA is designed to design.

That's part of the whole reinvention God does within us. He keeps molding and remolding us from one phase to another phase. Each step of reinvention is full of creativity and beauty. Each season of our life for a specific purpose. Nothing wasted through the reinventing process.

Keep your eye out for Apple Orchard Lane products. You never know. Why have I held on to that name for over forty years? Is it that God has future plans for me that he hasn't revealed yet that will incorporate my Apple Orchard Lane name? I will keep daydreaming about ideas, and perhaps one day those dreams will be fleshed out. I'm starting to rethink my Meal Candles. Perhaps they could still work...

Instant Rice

Lately, I've been on an instant brown rice kick. I'm trying to 'up' the healthy eating factor in our home, and so brown rice was an easy change. Especially the fact that brown rice comes in an instant form. Even better. In four minutes, after popping water and rice in a microwave safe bowl you 'ta-da' have completed rice to serve your family. Completed brown rice. Healthier.

Since I'm talking rice, I must tell you that my absolute favorite is Rice-a-Roni 'The San Francisco Treat'. I honestly have the hardest time saying the name Rice-a-Roni without singing the complete jingle. What kind of Rice-a-Roni? Pretty much all the flavors. My favorite? Four Cheese. I love making the four cheese for homemade burritos and layered Mexican Bakes. Yummo. There's something wonderful about browning that rice in the butter, and watching the long-grains turn brown. That rice really is a treat!

A few weeks ago, I was on a health food store 'kick', so I bought "real" brown rice. I thought it would just take a few minutes to cook up. When I read the directions a few minutes prior to cooking the rice, I was surprised to read that it had to boil for thirty minutes. Now my whole meal timing was off. Real rice takes longer. The more real the rice, the longer it takes to cook.

Dreams, goals, and visions we have for our lives are sometimes like the rice I bought at the health food store. The more natural and healthier, the longer it can take to "cook". Rarely do dreams we have for our lives fall into the instant rice category.

I started speaking for women's events in the mid 1990's. We were living in Tulsa, Oklahoma, and I wanted to have a 'job' that gave me flexibility as a stay at home mom. My title of mom was my chosen career. I needed something to supplement that career choice.

I always thought that women's church groups were filled with old ladies. I grew up in a Presbyterian church, and the only women's 'ministries' we had were called circles. These women's circles were created for those who wanted to quilt, sew, or make Christmas ornaments for the Chrismon Tree in the sanctuary each year at The First Presbyterian Church in New Brunswick, New Jersey. They made Chrismon ornaments, or knit blankets for shut-ins. Now don't get me wrong. Ornaments and blankets are important.

I don't want to cause a 'stir' in any circles!

There might have also been a 'Bridge Circle' in my Presbyterian church. You know those Presbyterians, they never did have problems with playing cards! I actually don't see any problem with cards, either, but that discussion belongs in another book.

The only women who were a part of those circles were old. At least it seemed that way when I was growing up. Women's Ministry was a lot different back in the 70's and early 80's.

So in the mid 90's, when I thought about what I could do to bring in extra income, I thought that perhaps I could do some speaking for women's ministry banquets and events. I had done concerts with my husband and groups for years, but I had never done a solo speaking event. Could I? What would I speak on?

I brainstormed, and realized that I had a heart for hospitality. We loved having people in our home, and after so many years of staying in host homes, I knew what I liked and didn't like in terms of hospitality. I could write a book alone on host home stories. Perhaps I will someday. In the Dewey Decimal System, you could categorize a book on staying in host homes in the Horror/Comedy section.

So I had my topic. I came up with the name Real Life Hospitality. In the 1990's that was fairly cutting edge. Fairly. The name fit my heart and theme. Hospitality for real life.

I typed up my notes. I designed a brochure that

looked like a mini newspaper that had 'articles' about hospitality, complete with a recipe for (fantastic) pumpkin bread. But I needed something 'catchy'. What would catch the eye of the women's ministry directors of the churches I sent this promotional piece to? I decided to put together a packet of the spices needed to make the pumpkin bread recipe. I bought mini-sized plastic baggies. Perfectly sized for two tablespoons of cinnamon, nutmeg, and pumpkin pie spice. That little packet smelled so good!

I bought a cute 'stamping stamp' of a pumpkin, bought parchment-looking paper, and fancy scissors that sculpted the edges beautifully when I cut the stamped pumpkin into a square piece. To attach the pumpkin square to the spice packet, I punched a mini hole in the pumpkin square, and attached it to the packet with a piece of ultra-thin craft rope tied in a bow. I hot glued the cute spice package to the promo piece, and had matching envelopes made. It was pretty darn cute. By the time the packet reached a church, the whole envelope was scented with pumpkin bread spices. Now who wouldn't love that scent?

I sent those packets out to area churches, and I started getting calls to come share my Real Life Hospitality presentation. My new career had started.

In those first years, I was happy to get any speaking engagement. My average pay for a speaking event then? About $300. And $300 per event was great additional income for a stay at home mom!

A door opened up for me to be able to speak as a break-out session speaker for a Hearts At Home Conference that was being held in town. This was a big deal. There were hundreds of women at this event, and I was to speak for two separate sessions. I was excited. I was starting to really enjoy speaking. This new career of mine was addicting. I wanted to do more and more speaking.

During one of the lunch breaks at the conference, one of the other break-out speakers asked me to lunch. We went across the street from the conference center, and enjoyed a nice meal together. She had been out speaking for a while, and I was mildly interrogating her as to how she got her speaking bookings.

"Well, God just opens up the doors," was her answer to how she received her bookings. That's all she told me. Plain and simple.

What? That's it? I wanted more info. The specifics of how, please. How did churches contact you? How do you get your name out? How do you get out of state bookings? I had so much I wanted to learn. I wanted more detail than 'God just opens up doors'.

My parents taught me that if you wanted something, you had to work hard for it. 'We were given a brain, and we can't just sit and expect God to do everything for us' was a resonating work ethic in our home. I understood that God was ultimately the one who opens up doors, but we needed to do our part. That's what I was trying to find out. How do you get from just a few speaking events to being booked on a regular basis? I didn't receive that "magical equation" for getting speaking bookings that day. No instant rice answer.

So let's jump to the present. It's been years since my lunch date with the fellow Hearts At Home speaker. I'm not saying I have all the answers now. Far from it. I wish I had discovered a magical equation for speaking bookings, but my journey has been a lot like that health store rice I purchased. Sometimes it takes a lot longer than you expect.

There are a few miracle stories of instant fame and recognition in this world. A Few. Most people just keep plugging away. I (usually) make more than $300 per speaking event now, and most of the speaking engagements I have, I get flown to. It's also taken me over sixteen years to get to this point. Is this it? No way. I still have gobs more I want to accomplish speaking-wise. My personal 'vision board' in my office is chock full. I plan on doing this till the day I journey out of this world. I still have so much more to learn!

Have you heard the saying, "I've paid my dues", or "You have to pay your dues". Well, that really is part of life. 'Dues' are your stepping stones. Dues are where you learn.

I have paid some dues. I enjoy where I am in life right now, but I've had years of 'dues'.

When I toured with the group, Re-Creation, I had a very prominent and important position. Yup, that's right, I was the monitor girl! Sounds important, doesn't it? Well, what my job actually consisted of was checking the placement of the monitors and speakers, and most importantly, running the cords. That's right. My responsibility was to make sure that the monitor and speaker cords were run correctly, and especially that they were taped properly. My best friend that year was gray duct tape. And yes, it is duct, not duck. So many call it DUCK tape. Novices.

I not only made sure the cords were run and taped in a perfectly aligned fashion, I also had to untape the cords after the show, and wrap up all of those sound cords in a neat and orderly manner. I took pride in my side job. I sang and was a 'show girl', and after the glamor and applause, I was back to cord rolling. Paying my dues. There are advantages. I know some 'techie' stuff now. Hiring me to speak for a retreat, but need some sound cords run? I'm your girl. Trust me, those cords will look fabulous.

The year before I married Dave, I toured in Larnelle Harris' back-up group, Friends. Our first big tour with Larnelle was a Christmas Tour. We had sets, and stage decorations. Yes, I was a singer, and enjoyed singing 'Amen' every night with Larnelle, but my side gig? Setting up and tearing down that delightful set. Every night. We had white lit snowmen placed across the whole stage. The snowmen were lit with dozens of little white light bulbs. Those light bulbs had to be screwed in every snowman before the concert, and screwed out, then placed back in special boxes every night. Every concert. Dues.

I do want to give a shout out to Larnelle Harris. Larnelle had proven himself, and paid his dues years before. Yet, he would help us disassemble the set decorations many nights. He would autograph every last record or photo, then come on stage and see if we still needed any help. He's a great man. He never got 'too big for his britches'. I love that about him.

Paying your dues is the opposite of entitlement. You realize that there are steps to becoming the vision of your dreams. I didn't look at rolling monitor cords or tearing down Christmas sets as a job that was 'lesser' than what I deserved. It's all a process. I know behind the scenes information, now. I could fill in for some techie jobs, if I had to. I was gaining wisdom along the way. It's part of the process of 'slow cooking that rice'. The longer and slower it cooks, the better the flavor and texture.

So what do you do in-between the inception of a dream, vision, or goal, and its fruition? What did I do since starting to speak in the 1990's, and now? A lot. I worked at doing all I could to be a better speaker and kept pursuing better booking avenues. I looked at every speaking opportunity as a way to improve my skills. I 'paid my dues' by accepting every speaking event that came my way. Instead of thinking, "That isn't enough money", I accepted, and was grateful for the open door. And I didn't give up on my dream.

On October 29th, 1941, the United Kingdom's Prime Minister, Winston Churchill, was asked to speak to the students of the Harrow School, where he had attended when he was a child. He gave the famous very short speech that people have quoted ever since. His words are my words to you today, "Never, ever, ever, ever, ever, ever, ever, give up. Never give up. Never give up. Never give up." Thank you, Mr. Churchill.

After struggling to develop a viable electric light-bulb for months and months, Thomas Edison was interviewed by a young reporter who boldly asked Mr. Edison if he felt like a failure and if he thought he should just give up by now. Perplexed, Edison replied, "Young man, why would I feel like a failure? And why would I ever give up? I now know definitively over 9,000 ways that an electric light bulb will not work. Success is almost in my grasp." And shortly after that, and over 10,000 attempts, Edison invented the light bulb.

Never give up.

Never giving up is step one. It's simple. Keep with your dream. Accept every step along the way as an opportunity to learn more. Work on your craft. Perfect it. Keep creating. Keep visualizing. Keep planning. Never give up.

"It's all about who you know" is another keeper of a saying. I hate to admit it, but it really is all about who you know. It's also an important realization in the fleshing out of your dream career, goal, or potential money making idea. There are innumerable people who have great ideas. But if you know people who can take your invention, and get it in the hands of the right people, you are 'giant steps' ahead of everyone else.

Personal example? Dave was in the well-known singing group, TRUTH. They were simply the best. Remember the songs 'Majesty' and 'Jesus Never Fails'? Well, my Davey sang on the original recordings of those songs. I know. I married someone famous. For five dollars I'll get you his autograph if you're interested. (He'll die when he reads this!)

Being part of the TRUTH family is an instant connection to so many talented musicians. Know the group 4HIM? They were all members of TRUTH. The song 'If You Could See Me Now'? Written by Kim Nobblit, who toured with Dave. The TRUTH world is a small world...after all.

How does Dave's TRUTH connections relate to me? A few years ago, Dave had lunch with the man who was their vocal and instrumental arranger for TRUTH's last five years on the road, Greg Wiggins. A brilliant musician and composer. If you are a TRUTH fan, he arranged all of the music for the Farewell Tour. Fantastic stuff. Dave was down in Mobile, Alabama producing a CD for a client. He had an afternoon off, and Roger Breland (the director of TRUTH) suggested that Dave have lunch with Greg. They met, had a great lunch, and stayed in touch.

A few weeks later, Greg was hired as the new Musical Director for Benny Hinn Ministries. He called Dave up and told him about his new position, and said that he needed to put together a Worship Team for a crusade that was happening in less than two weeks, and would Dave be available to sing with the group? I was sitting next to Dave on the couch during the call, and I gave him a big 'thumbs up' sign.

Dave and I were doing concerts every weekend together that year, so the additional income as well as ministry was a bonus. Later that evening, Greg called back and asked if I was also available to sing with the group. Double thumbs up on that one! We received 20+ songs in an email to learn for our first crusade in San Antonio in a week and a half!

That was almost six years ago, and we have been able to travel the country singing in arenas together, and even had the opportunity to travel to Israel for a 10-day trip of singing and filming a DVD of the Singers. What an amazing opportunity! The singers and band we sing with are seriously some of the best musicians in the country. The best musicians and the greatest friends.

Now, are there better singers in the world than myself? Yes! Are there better female soloists that could fill my spot with the group? In a heartbeat. Why am I up on stage singing with the group instead of them? Who we knew. Of course, we feel that God ordained all of our involvement with that ministry, but it was also the fact that Dave knew Roger Breland, who knew Greg Wiggins.

Now, getting in to the right place may be a matter of who you know, but how I've kept my position with the ministry is the fact that I have stepped up to the plate, and have done my 'job' well. I know what they need from me, and I fulfill that need to the best of my abilities. I give 110%.

Social media has been a fantastic networking tool. A networking tool, but also a wonderful medium to stay in touch with people. I've been able to connect with people on social networking sites, that I would never have been able to contact on my own. Again, it's a case of 'I know this person, and they know that person, so therefore, I am able to get in touch with that person because of this person'. Now if you understood that, raise your hand. Anyone?

Stay connected. Find creative ways to be connected with the people that are influential in the field that you want to be in. Do you want to write books? Get in touch with those that are published, and are actively writing. Do you want to form your own band some day? Contact these bands, and get on their fan pages. Find out about their lives. Find out how they got where they are today.

Now I'm not promoting stalking! Although at rare times, I may be slightly guilty of mild stalking. Social media allows for some of that, thank you very much.

Do you have an invention that you're wanting to get recognized? Research who's out there inventing, and find out all you can about them. Stay connected, and get connected with the movers and shakers in the field that you're interested in. Those are the people that (when you have been able to prove yourself) can open doors for you that you could never open yourself!

Now, the third point of my three point sermon. Well, this isn't really a sermon, but I wanted to sound dignified. In seminary they teach pastors to have three points to their sermons, and I just happened to be bringing you a third point to waiting out your dream.

What to do while your long-grain rice is cooking? Let's review. Never give up and get to know more people in your 'dream field', because a lot of making your dreams come true is who you know. Now to the third and final point.

#3 Never burn your bridges.

Now if you have a literal bridge that you own, this is a given. Especially if you have one of those New England-type beautiful red and white picturesque bridges. Do you own one of those? Never burn it. Please.

OK, seriously. Don't burn your bridges=don't dismiss past relationships. Don't walk away from a relationship in your life in a mean-spirited fashion. Now please understand me, if you have been in an abusive relationship, that is a totally different situation from what I am referring to right now. Abusive, bad, unsafe, unhealthy relationships? YES, walk away from those and don't go back.

In reference to not burning bridges, I am talking about people that have been or are presently in your life. Say, for example, for whatever reason, you leave a job. That boss, and all the people you worked with are people that you need to keep an open relationship with. Do you need to picnic every weekend together? No. I am advising, whatever the circumstances for leaving the job, that you do your utmost to keep the relationship lines open. Don't bad mouth that boss on your way out. Don't make comments like, "Well, GOODBYE! You were the worst boss EVER!" and slam the door.

You know what will happen? That next position that you interview for will ask about your previous job. They'll want the name and previous phone number of your previous boss as a reference. Oh, and they'll call him/her, too. If you were ugly on your way out, that's the image that your boss will retain. That's the reference that your new possible boss will hear.

Don't burn the bridge.

We have worked in various churches in our twenty-one years of being married. Well, let me correct that statement. Dave has been the one churches have hired, but I'm kind of included in that hiring 'package'. If you have worked in church ministry, you know what I'm saying. Husband and wife is a two-for-one deal. I'm not being ugly, just that when you hire one, you are really getting both people. Both are (or should be) highly involved together.

We had a church position (I will be a lady and not disclose the name of the church) where we had a rough departing scenario. We had been at this church for a year. It was a bit of a rough year. We walked in as newbies, and within a month, there was a church split! The Administrator of the church had been embezzling funds (at least that was the story we heard). Apparently he had a good amount of followers that believed his side of the story, and left the church with him.

Have you ever walked through a church split? Tough times. Especially when you are a brand new staff member. Dave had been brought in as a 'change man' to transition the music department. Again, there could be a whole book written on a 'church music transitioner'! So when the split took place, the transition stopped. The pastor wanted the music back to the way it had been for years. It's a long crazy story. We walked though that craziness for a year, and headed out to California for a week of vacation to visit with Dave's family.

Five days into our vacation, Dave called back to the church to just check in with the pastor, and let him know we were good. What Dave heard on the phone was a shock!

"Well, I thought you were out interviewing for another church. I've interviewed a couple of guys for your position, and already hired one."

WHAT?!?!?! WE WERE JUST OUT VACATIONING! The pastor had HIRED someone else? What??? The worst part? He asked Dave to keep that information to himself. "I need you to tell people that it was your idea to leave. I don't want anyone from the church knowing that I hired someone while you were away."

Unbelievable, huh? I know! Our boys were just little then, too. Tyler was barely three, and Ryan had just turned one. Where in the world were we going to go? Our job was terminated in a very shady way, and yet we were to be all smiles for the congregation when we went back? How unfair was that?

Yet, we decided to take the high road, as hard as it was. We left that church with our dignity. I had those matches and gasoline in hand, and was so ready to set that bridge in a burning inferno! Buh-BYE! Don't ever want to see you AGAIN! But we couldn't do it.

The churches that hired us in following years all called that pastor for a reference. And because of how we left that church, Dave always received a 'glowing' reference from that pastor. Would it have been easy to have bad-mouthed that pastor to everyone in that church? Yes. Could it have caused another church split? Possibly. Was it worth it? No.

We have put forth the effort, and sometimes it takes a lot of effort to leave places and jobs with dignity and character without being spiteful and ugly. Burning a bridge is easy. A little gasoline and a match will do the job. Ka-Boom. It's gone. Maintaining a bridge takes a lot of work. You must keep up with repairs, and repaint when needed. If the wood is rotting, it must be replaced or fixed. Work? Yes, but worth it in the long run.

Never giving up, keeping and making connections

with people, and not burning your bridges are ingredients for reinventing yourself into who you want to be, and for seeing your dreams materialize. Slow process? Sometimes. Worth seeing your dream come alive?

Yep.

Now go melt some butter on that rice and season it up.

Buh-Bye Now

I love flying. I usually have at least two destinations a month to which I have to fly. Problem? Nope. It makes me smile every time I get on a plane! Planes are missing a key ingredient in the recent years, though: the airplane meal.

It used to be the highlight of your flight. What was the meal that would be served? I remember boarding a plane and trying to figure out what the lunch or dinner was by just the smell. Then the wait came. Watching other rows get served made us the epitome of Pavlov's dog. "Did you see what it is yet? What are the choices? I hope they haven't run out of the one I want."

Oh, and once you saw what the two choices of meal were, it was major decision time. The lasagna or the chicken with wild rice? I loved the mini drinks, the mini salads, the mini rolls, the mini desserts, mini salt packets, mini pepper packets, and the mini butters. Loved. Them. All.

Now what do they do? They serve you a teensy bag of pretzels. Those bags, if you're lucky, have 13 pretzels in them. And if you want to buy a snack/meal, it'll cost you eight dollars! Who's idea was it to delete the meal? They so should have just upped the ticket price and kept the meal. People would have been happier. People liked to be fed on a plane. Plane rides went by so much faster with the meal serving. Sad days we live in.

I always like to be courteous on an airplane exit. What makes me really happy? To be able to see the pilot and say, "Thank you for keeping us safe". Mama raised me right. I know my manners.

I also enjoy how the attendants (I will go old school and call them the right names; Stewards and Stewardesses—again another change that didn't need to happen) say good-bye to every single passenger. That's a tradition that should never change, thank you very much.

Have you seen the Saturday Night Live skit with Helen Hunt and David Spade as the airplane stewardess and steward? It's a classic. It's funny. Everyone is exiting the plane, and all they say to each passenger is, "Buh-Bye". Different passengers have complaints, or want help, and all they keep saying is, "Buh-Bye. Buh-Bye. Buh-Bye."

Now when I exit and hear the same "Buh-Bye" out

of the real-life, non-Saturday Night Life characters, it makes me chuckle on the inside. They must get tired of saying "Buh-Bye" to everyone.

I have struggled as to where I should place this chapter in the book. The beginning wouldn't have been right, yet I didn't want to depress you by placing it at the end. So, it's here. Randomly placed for your reading pleasure. It won't be a long chapter, but it's a necessary one.

WHEN YOU SHOULD SAY BUH-BYE

This isn't going to be fun for some of you. I'm telling you ahead of time. You've been warned. It's a hard pill to swallow for some, but hopefully this chapter will prove to be 'good medicine'.

Are you still with me? Have you tossed the book to the ground yet?

Some of you want to be someone you weren't created to be. You want to be reinvented into your personal 'dream version' of yourself. But that isn't who God designed you to be. Let me gently explain.

My husband has been a Worship Pastor on and off for the past twenty five years of our marriage. I think I've already told you that a dozen times in this book. Just a quick reiteration. Over those years of working with church choirs and praise teams, he's only had a handful of volunteers who were sweet, sweet souls, but perhaps would be better off giving of themselves in a different ministry.

I know I'm walking on egg shells here, but I will continue. We deal in a very visible ministry of the church. I'm not saying the music department is better, just more visible. There are many ministries in the church where people go unnoticed, and my hats off to them. They are generous givers of their time and talents, and rarely get a thank you. I am acknowledging you now. The church couldn't run without all of you.

But, on the flip side, the music loft is right up front and center every Sunday morning. And we are mic'd, mic'ed, miked(?). We are on microphones. I looked up the proper spelling for 'mic'd', and I got all three spellings, so I wanted to give all of you proper spellers the opportunity to choose which spelling you would prefer to read.

Spellings aside, there are microphones surrounding the music loft on every side, and some coming down from the ceiling. We are heard. We are magnified. If you cough or clear your throat, the whole congregation hears you. I know this from experience. Also, while in the choir loft, be careful what you say about what people are wearing that Sunday. They can hear that, too. Trust me.

We can literally count on one hand the times where Dave has had to intervene, and gently encourage someone to serve in another area of ministry other than the choir. He's a gentle, loving soul, that man of mine. He's so good with people.

My Dave is such a great music ministry recruiter.

He's always encouraging people in the church to join the choir. I love him for that. One Wednesday night we had a new man show up in the bass section. He was warmly welcomed and received, and we were thrilled to have another low voice.

A few rehearsals into this new man's choir tenure, Dave knew he had a problem. This man was completely tone deaf. This man was also a very strong singer. Timid he was not.

The people around our newest choir member could not hear themselves sing. They couldn't keep their own right notes. We had a problem.

He was being mic'd, mic'ed, miked. Under those microphones, his tone deafness and volume was even more pronounced. Now what to do?

Not that my husband couldn't work with someone like that. He has, and he probably will again. The problem was the volume, and the fact that it was throwing the whole choir off. It was actually distracting from the worship, which is vitally important in a service. If people are distracted by that 'loud off sound', they aren't able to enter into worship. This one gentleman, in particular, Dave knew, needed to be ushered from the choir to work with, well, possibly the ushers themselves!

My husband finally had to do something. He took his newest choir member out to lunch. It was probably to Chipotle. Dave loves that place. What's not to love about Chipotle. Huge chicken, beef, or pork burritos stuffed with cilantro rice, black beans, pico de gallo, sour cream, cheese, lettuce, and guacamole. (That's actually what I order on my chicken burrito from there.) It's uh-mazing. I want one now.

So Dave took this sweet man out to lunch. He encouraged him that perhaps there was another ministry better suited to his giftings. That was one of the most difficult things Dave ever had to do. Thank the Lord it doesn't happen much.

Even though this man had a heart for singing in the choir, he would not be living in the fullness of who he was created to be, if he had stayed in that position. How do I know that's not where he was supposed to be, you may ask? I have a checklist. Again, I don't want you to look at this chapter as discouraging, but rather encouraging. Perhaps you've been living for years thinking that your talent is one thing, when it's actually something completely different. Only when you realize it might be time to move on, will you finally walk in your proper place of gifting.

Here's a little personal example before I delve into the checklist.

Since I have been singing for so many years, people just naturally assume that I also write songs. I don't. Well, not really. I have actually written a few songs, but they haven't been officially published. Yet. The first song I wrote? Shampoo. That's right, it's a song about shampooing that I would sing for my boys when I was giving them baths when they were little.

SHAMPOO
by
Kirsten Hart

Shampoo
Shampoo
I love to Shampoo
I love to Shampoo
How 'bout you?

Now I'm quite sure that if you heard the tune that accompanied my in-depth lyrics, you would appreciate my song writing abilities that much more.

What was that? Did I just hear you request another one of my songs? Why, you're so sweet!

DEAD SKUNK
by
Kirsten Hart

Dead skunk
Dead skunk
Dead skunk in the middle of the road
Dead skunk
Dead skunk
Dead skunk in the middle of the road.

I know you'd never guess it, but that song was

inspired while we lived and toured full time in our motor home. Guess we saw a lot of dead skunks that were in the middle of the road that year.

An *Encore?* Why you people are just too kind. Please keep in mind that the following song, (as well as 'Dead Skunk') really does need to be heard rather than just read. The tunes are quite catchy, if I may say so myself. Here is my third and final song:

MAGICAL WORLD
by
Kirsten Hart

We live in a magical world
We live in a magical world
We live in a magical
Live in a magical
Live in a magical
World.

I used to sing 'Magical World' to my son Ryan in the mornings, as I drove him to Ridgeview Elementary School, when he was in 4th grade. Granted not every day. Close, though. 'Magical World' would then be stuck in my head all day long. It may not seem like a Top 30 Countdown song, but those lyrics and tunes can get stuck!

So my point is? Other than sharing my delightful lyrics with you? Song writing is not my gift. Even though I sing, and would love to have that gift, I have come to realize it's not who I was created to be. I'm not ruling out the possibility that when I'm in my 80's, God might decide to reinvent in me the gift of lyrics and melodies, but in my forty-eight years of living, this gift has not shown itself to be worthy. I'm OK with that. I understand that everyone doesn't and won't have the same gifts and abilities in this world.

Although Magical World could still be a hit someday...would I love to write songs? Sure! How do I know it's not what I'm supposed to do? *A-ha.* Here comes the checklist.

HOW TO KNOW WHEN TO SAY 'BUH-BYE' TO WHAT YOU THOUGHT YOU WANTED AND WERE GOOD AT, WHEN IT'S NOT WHO YOU WERE CREATED TO BE CHECKLIST:

Have you had positive responses from people? Have people received you well? I don't mean do people *like* you, but have people responded to your ideas, dreams, or what you perceive as your giftings in a positive way?

This is all so general, so I'm going to give a specific example, and base my checklist on that example alone. Fill in the following scenario with your own idea, dream, goal.

Let's take a familiar scenario. There are umpteen TV shows based on this scenario: You Want To Become A Famous Singer. Let's say that this has always been your dream. You, like so many, feel that you are really good at singing, and you are ready for your big break, and can't understand why that hasn't happened yet in your life. OK, now back to the checklist's #1 question.

Have you had positive responses from people?

Hello! So you want to be a famous singer, do you? You want a recording contract, and to make millions of dollars as a singer? Well, congratulations!

How have people responded to your singing talents? You may be a karaoke singer. Some karaoke singers are great. Some are horrible. It all depends on who is listening. If you have sung karaoke with a bunch of crazy college kids who think karaoke is a fun way to kill a boring Friday night and you won the night's 'Trophy', congratulations. Have you been able to sing those same songs in front of a crowd that has some musical background, and has been involved in the music industry themselves? Whole different group. Whole different viewpoint.

What has been the general response of those hearing your singing? Have they said you have a nice, voice? (*Nice* is usually a people-friendly term meaning 'you're not really good, but I don't want to hurt your feelings, so I'll say the word, nice'.) Nice is really only a word that should be used to describe a sweet old grandma. It's a nondescript compliment. Have you heard that word a lot in regards to your singing?

If people haven't complimented you on your singing abilities, or just haven't said anything to you, it's a good inclination that singing may not be your proper gift. Now, sometimes family members wrongly encourage those who think they are gifted, but really aren't. Just because Aunt Josephine thinks you're the best singer since Johnny Cash doesn't necessarily mean that you are destined for a recording contract by Christmas.

It fascinates me to watch some of the singing talent competitions on TV. Some of those people are horrible singers, yet adamantly claim that they are so much better than even the judges themselves. Absolutely clueless.

I don't ever want you to be clueless. What's the opposite of clueless? Clueful? Probably aware, or the fancier term cognizant would be a better fit, but I kind of like the term clueful. I'm keeping it. Even though my computer has placed a red line under the word, signifying that clueful is a massive misspelling. Clueful, clueful, clueful. My favorite brand new word.

If you have had wonderful positive feedback for your singing abilities, than that is a signal that you're on the right track. Keep plugging away. Congratulations.

Have you been at it for years without anything happening?

Now don't get me wrong. I know in a previous chapter, I encouraged you to never, ever, ever, ever give up. Well, I may change my tune for just a moment.

If you have abandoned regular, everyday life to pursue your dream of being a singer, and nothing has happened your whole life, it may be time to move on to something else. Perhaps God isn't reinventing you into *that* particular field. You need to tune in to what God is doing in the reinvention process of your life. Perhaps he has a different path. Tune into him. Read his word. Dig in to God's heart, and listen for the direction he is leading you towards.

I have met people that are only dreamers and 'wanters', and live in sort of a fantasy world that they are going to be stars. There comes a time when, if you're at a certain age, and if it hasn't happened yet, that it may be too late. I'm not trying to be a Negative Nancy here, just more of a realist. If you're 65, and always wanted to be Donny Osmond, you may want to rethink your career goals. That ship may have sailed years ago.

Now you may think I'm exaggerating with the Donny Osmond scenario, but you may be surprised. I've met many that were beyond their 'teen idol' years, that still wanted to be teen idols! Perhaps they could be 'Senior Idols'. Now there's a whole new genre waiting to be opened!

You see what I'm saying, though, right? If you're past the age of being on the Mickey Mouse Club, and that's what you always wanted, perhaps you could create a new dream goal for your life. A more realistic one. The past is the past, and it's gone. If you haven't been able to accomplish what you wanted, then it may be time for something new! New isn't so bad! New can be even better!

Don't get stuck in the mire of old, dilapidated dreams for yourself. God may be on to something new and wonderful for you, but you can't let go of your grasp on your old dream. Perhaps it's time to say 'Buh-Bye', but in your next breath, say 'Hello' to something fresh and exciting.

Do you walk in peace and prosperity?

How do you know if God is part of what you are doing? I believe with all my heart that if God is the one directing your life, that peace and prosperity will be right by your side. Don't get me wrong, I'm not saying that you'll be a walking millionaire. (Although that would be amazing).

Where God is, there is peace. If you are following in your God-given abilities, and walking out the steps he has planned for you, you will have peace. A deep peace, that you know you are where you should be, doing what you were created to do. Peace is such a vital element of being smack dab in the middle of your giftings. I can almost guarantee you, that if your life-long dream has always been to make it as a singer, and you are living life uneasy, and troubled, then you need to change directions.

Is your family not at peace because you're still trying to make your dream come true? Is there unrest and tension caused by what you want, instead of what God actually has in mind for your life? No dream is worth a family existing in a non-peace-filled state.

Prosperity? Yes. Prosperity in the sense that you are able to make ends meet financially, and that God is blessing what you are doing.

I see them all the time. The wanna be rocker dudes. They grew up in the 60's and 70's, and always wanted to make it big in a band. They never did, but they haven't given up the dream. So, they play with their garage rock bands at every bar gig in town making pennies every night, but hoping that some agent will see them perform, and they might still get signed, and have a record deal.

Meanwhile, the families of these guys are barely getting by. They can't pay the bills, and can barely feed the children. They're holding on to a dead dream, and not being financially responsible to their duties as husbands, fathers, and as responsible, bill-paying citizens. Do you know someone like this?

I don't mean to come down so harsh, but this is a reality chapter. Prosperity is an interesting word. To some it's a positive word, to others, a negative. I want you to look at it in a positive light. If you are where you should be with the proper gifts and abilities that are yours, you should be prospering—at least able to pay your bills!

I don't believe that God desires for us, his children, to be struggling through this world, and to be irresponsible financially. If your personal pursuit of a dream is causing your family to suffer, it may be time to put the guitar away, and get a job/career where you can still use your gifts, but you can also put food on the table and shoes on the kids.

Am I saying to sell your guitar, or give up on

singing? No. Especially if that is something your thoroughly enjoy. But you may need to give up the record deal dream. If the only paycheck you bring home is from the tip jar at the Karaoke bar, you may need to rethink your career calling.

This is all kind of harsh, isn't it? It's kind of a rough chapter for me to write. I love being an encourager. But as a mom, I also see the importance of tough love. This chapter is my tough love chapter. But remember, there is love behind every word I'm writing. I desire for you to thrive in your life. Thrive with peace and prosperity, and joy, and a happy family and life. You can have all of that; when you live out your dreams and reinventions with intelligence and responsibility.

Some of you may have to say 'Buh-Bye' to an old washed out dream. Remember, God is the giver of dreams and visions. If you have been holding on firmly to a dream you've always had for yourself, but it has never come to life, perhaps God is just waiting to give you new vision, and a better dream. A new dream that is better than you could have ever imagined for yourself.

God will reinvent you, but *not* into someone you weren't originally *meant* to be. There is a flow to your 'river of life', it will all fit together perfectly. But don't get so stuck on the idea of who *you* think you want to be, that God can't mold you into that beautiful vision he has for your future.

See. I'm going to end this chapter on a positive note. The best is yet to come! The stewardess may be saying 'Buh-Bye' to you, but once you exit that plane, you have a whole new wonderful destination in front of you, just waiting to be explored!

DREAM CAPSULE

In preparation for this chapter, I researched the history of time capsules. I thought they had been around forever. Apparently, the first time capsule was created in 1935, and it was actually a time room, to be preserved and unopened until the year 8113 A.D. That's a long time from now.

"In 1935, while engaged in research on ancient historical materials in connection with the writing of one of his books, Dr. Thornwell Jacobs, then President of Oglethorpe University, Atlanta, Georgia, was struck by the lack of accurate information regarding ancient civilizations. Determined to make an effort to preserve in a scientific manner every salient feature of present day civilization for the people of the future, Dr. Jacobs devised the plans for the Crypt of Civilization. Looking back to the first recorded date in history about 6000 years ago, he decided to set the opening of the vault on May 28, about 6000 years hence, in the year 8113 A.D.

To assist him in this tremendous task, Dr. Jacobs sought the help of Thomas K. Peters, a scientist of versatile experience. Work on the Crypt commenced in August, 1937, and continued until June, 1940. During this period of thirty-three months, an astounding amount of knowledge was condensed: the accumulated knowledge acquired during the 72,000 months of the last 6000 years."

This was, in fact, a crypt. More than just a capsule. It contained just about everything related to 1937. Pretty cool!

At the World's Fair of 1939, the first actual 'capsule' was placed in a shaft that descended fifty feet below Flushing Meadows Park in Queens, New York. It's still there, too! Alongside the 1939 capsule is the time capsule from the 1964 World's Fair. (Now if you have heard my story, or read my book Baby Girl Murphy, you'll know that I was conceived during the 1964-1965 World's Fair in NYC).

Although these are the first recorded time capsules/crypts, the Egyptians were really the first ones to perfect this art. Even though what they were preserving was for their afterlife, they were amazing at preserving aspects of everyday life in Egypt, and left for us literal treasure chests full of glimpses into what life in Egypt was like thousands of years ago. Archeology and History books would be missing dozens of pages, had the Egyptians not prepared so intricately for their next life.

Time capsules kind of fascinate me. I wonder who in the future will open these frozen fragments of life, and what their reactions will be. Will future generations wait as long as the time capsule recommends? Will they be anxious, and open them early? Will those buried capsules be covered up and forgotten?

I vaguely remember a time capsule project at my Johnson Park Elementary School in Princeton, New Jersey. We always had gym class in the cafeteria, but during second grade, they started construction on the brand new gymnasium.

The word spread throughout school that they were putting together a time capsule to place in the cornerstone of the new gym. If I recall correctly, some of the artistically gifted students even had their artwork added to the time capsule. Luckies. I wonder what other 1970's memorabilia is contained in there? I hope they at least got a Malibu Barbie! And to be fair to the boys, a G.I. Joe.

Time capsules give future generations all the information relevant to the past. They are glimpses into what was important and what the current knowledge, trends, fashion, and scientific knowledge was at the time the capsules were sealed. Don't open them before their time, either. No peeking! That information is to be preserved for a particular year and time in this world.

God sends us our own time capsules. He knows the appointed seasons in our lives for us to discover buried knowledge. Perhaps he has new life giftings for us, but we have to wait until just the right time in our lives to open those hidden treasures. He has a time and place for us to open these specially designed dream capsules, and they are preserved for us at specific times.

I never dreamed that public speaking would be a part of my life, but at the right time, God gave me a 'capsule' to open, and my gift of speaking was inside, along with all the tools necessary to bring that gift into realization. The fact that you're reading a book that I wrote is another example of a 'gift capsule'. I never imagined that I would want to, or have the desire to write books. It was just within the past few years that I began to write. God unlocked and opened a 'gift/dream capsule' of writing in my life. It's an unexpected desire, but God knew that it was the right time in my life for me to develop writing abilities. It's really fascinating and wonderful how God works.

Ecclesiastes 3:1 says, "There is an appointed time for everything. And there is a time for every event under heaven."

I like to imagine that Heaven is full of gift and dream capsules. God waiting in Heaven for just the exact season in our life to send us that package of gifts and dreams. Has this happened to you? Are you involved in something in your life that you never thought you would be a part of, but yet now couldn't imagine your life without? I believe God creates us with everything we will be in life at conception. Yet there are still hidden talents and gifts that he has yet to reveal to us. When we are in tune with him, and open to all that God has for us, that's when the capsules of reinvention start arriving.

Sometimes we have years of preparation before we are ready to receive our dream capsules. There are different seasons in our lives, and different disbursements of gifts and dreams appropriate for each season.

If God had given me the capsule of public speaking when my boys were infants, I don't think I would have been as good of a mom to them. My heart would have been with my dream of speaking, and not with being a mother. I would have been pining for being out speaking, instead of being content at home with my sons. God did give me a heart for motherhood, and I basked in that gift and desire, and cherished my time and dream of being at home with my babies.

When our boys got older, and were in school all day, my 'speaking time capsule' arrived. I had a newly enhanced dream of being a full-time mother, as well as a speaker. It was the right time for that. I could take a few Saturdays a month to go out and speak without jeopardizing my calling as a stay-at-home mom.

Now don't get me wrong, I'm not trying to wage a war against working moms, I'm just speaking about my own personal experience. Remember, not everyone receives the same gift/dream capsules! They are created individually. Everyone has their own season and timing to be reinvented.

I am walking in a new season as I am writing this book. My oldest son is now married, and our youngest is in college. My 'writing capsule' arrived just in time for the empty nest. It's interesting that God didn't even start to reveal the writing interest in my life until this season. Why didn't he give it to me earlier? I don't know. I just trust in his perfect timing. As Ecclesiastes states, there is an appointed time for everything.

"I rejoice therefore that I have confidence in you in all things." What a great verse from 2 Corinthians 7:16. We can have confidence that God does, in fact, know what he's doing. There is no randomness to our lives. God knows and sees our future, and will give us our gifts and dreams at the perfect time in our lives. Trust that. Trust Him.

Are you waiting for your dream capsule to arrive? Does it feel like it has been lost in shipping? Are you wondering why your gifts and dreams are taking so long to get to you?

The mystery of seasons in our lives is one that is complex and intricate. Often times it feels like we are stuck in that preparation season. That season of anticipation. As if the tree is decorated, and yet Christmas morning never comes. Waiting on the Lord is a mystery. We don't know God's ways and reasons. If you are in a season of waiting, hold on to these wonderful verses:

"God can do anything, you know - far more than you could ever imagine or guess or request in your wildest dreams! He does it not by pushing us around but by working within us, his Spirit deeply and gently within us."--Ephesians 3:20

"No one's ever seen or heard anything like this, Never so much as imagined anything quite like it-- What God has arranged for those who love him." --I Corinthians 2:9

I just quoted two of my absolute favorite Bible verses. Aren't they encouraging? I love them! Repeat them to yourself time after time, until they're a part of you.

When is your dream capsule coming? At just the right time. Are you ready for a new capsule to come your way? Be patient, and live life to the fullest in the season you are in. Realize that sometimes the season of preparation is longer that we expect or desire.

There is reason and purpose in those times of preparation. Perhaps the right person hasn't walked into your life yet. Perhaps someone else has to get *themselves* prepared in order for your dream to come alive. Don't doubt. Keep trusting.

Galatians 6:9 is such a great verse to keep close to your heart if you are getting discouraged, or feel that God has forgotten to send your dream capsule. Keep your faith, hold on to the dreams God has given you, and live in anticipation of what's to come.

"So let's not allow ourselves to get fatigued doing good. At the right time we will harvest a good crop if we don't give up, or quit. "

So. Be. It.

LET'S HEAR IT FOR THE BOYS

So I realize this book is written by a woman, but this woman has been married to her man for over twenty-four years, and this woman has given birth to, and raised two young men. So, I wanted to focus in on the guys for just a few pages. I'm sure there isn't one woman who will skip over this chapter, either, by the way. We girls are always fascinated by boys. What makes you tick? In what ways in particular are we different? What do men *really* want in life?

I would win the Nobel Peace Prize if I had *all* the answers to those questions. But I don't. What do I have to offer? Some wisdom and guy encouragement. One thing I have learned about guys? They thrive on verbal recognition and praise. Not in a prideful manner, girls. It's just the way they're wired. Most women need hugs and kisses, men need verbal affirmation. Men, am I right? Let me try to *speak* some words of recognition and praise into your lives.

The two biggest decision factors in a man's life are: Who will I marry, and What will be my vocation. The two biggies. Who you will marry is a fun one, though, don't you think? Out of all the women in the world, you get the thrill of the hunt in finding just the right one. It's all about the hunt. What a delightful quest.

The second biggest decision is what will be your vocation. There is a lot of career pressure on men. Men, in general, are thought of as the bread winners. The ones who go out and work all day to bring home a paycheck, and to take care of their families. Now, I realize that times are different, and there are a lot of women who are the primary bread winners these days, but *typically* it is the man's role.

Talk of dreams and visions are part of a man's life, but so many times the primal need for food, shelter, and money override a man's personal dreams and goals. They are forced into doing what's needed, instead of what they would *love* to do.

I know women think they have a lot of pressure in their college years, but I don't believe it's as great as the pressure men have. They are given four years to decide who they will be for the rest of their lives. Their career choice decides the life they will lead and the income level they will live at. Some men have additional years to achieve their master's and

KirsTen HarT

doctorate levels of schooling, but after that is accomplished, it's time to work and provide for the rest of their lives. If they're lucky (and Social Security is still in place) they may possibly stop doing that chosen career at the age of sixty-five.

Men don't have a lot of room for dreaming of different careers, and exploring how they might want to change their career goals after college. How does a man go about finding what his dream career is?

Many times the pressure comes from his parents. Parents have high expectations for their sons. In my generation, boys were encouraged to be doctors or lawyers. Those were the sought after, primary career choices for someone who would make their parents proud. Today, parents might aspire for their sons to be wealthy entrepreneurs, computer programmers, or engineers.

If one's parents aren't forcing them into a particular career choice, how does someone know what they should become? If you are a father, how should you encourage your son in his career choice? Here are some examples of how someone can find what they're good at:

David's gifts are for inspiring people and leadership, and his passion is for football. His true vocation might be becoming a football coach.

Joe's gifts are in teaching and researching, and his passion is history. His true vocation might be becoming a history professor.

Dan's gifts are in resolving disputes, and his

passion is for making divorces more amicable for the partners and easier on kids. His true vocation might be becoming a divorce lawyer who concentrates on peaceful mediation.

Alex's gifts are in investigating things, and his passion is for animals and the outdoors. His true vocation might be becoming a game warden.

Tyler's gifts are in selling things and making deals, and his passion is for books. His true vocation might be becoming a literary agent.

Blake's gifts are in crunching numbers, and his passion is for politics. His true vocation might be becoming the state treasurer.

Dave's gifts are in language, and his passion is for Japan and Japanese culture. His true vocation might be becoming a translator in Japan.

Know your child well. What does he *love* to do? What is he naturally good at? What are his innate passions? What natural abilities does your son show? Instead of forcing him into a career choice he has no giftings for, discover what his natural God-given abilities are, and then focus a career from there. Or are you at a crossroads in life? Go through the above points, and think about yourself. Are you ready and able to branch out into something new? How do you decide what *your* new career should be?

New careers can be fun. You can rediscover who you always wanted to be. What passion did you lose when you jumped into the workforce? Did you lose who you *were* in order to receive a paycheck? There's nothing wrong at all with doing what you have to do to provide. But if you're fortunate enough to rebuild and reinvent for yourself, go for it.

I believe that most men know deep down what their calling is, what they really wish to do in life. The truly hard part is overcoming the obstacles and rationalizations we have for not following our callings.

Steve Jobs, the co-founder of Apple, and revolutionary visionary just recently passed away. He is a prime example of following your heart and your dreams. Even though he dropped out of college, he had the dream to make computers available in homes. A dream that at the time was unheard of. One of my favorite Steve Jobs' quotes is this:

"Your time is limited, so don't waste it living someone else's life. Don't be trapped by dogma — which is living with the results of other people's thinking. Don't let the noise of others' opinions drown out your own inner voice. And most important, have the courage to follow your heart and intuition. They somehow already know what you truly want to become."

Believe for yourself that the best years are still to come. If you are given the chance, live out your dreams. You only pass through this life once. You are given one chance to be who you were created to be. Don't walk through life unfulfilled, or doing what someone *else* thought you should do. Be wise, but live your life full. Be an inspiration to those around you. Inspire others to walk in their callings.

Being a leader in your home means leading by example. If you are living your life fulfilled, most likely your children will, too. Your spouse will be happier because you are happier, and you will enjoy life to its fullest.

"When I was 17, I read a quote that went something like: "If you live each day as if it was your last, someday you'll most certainly be right." It made an impression on me, and since then, for the past 33 years, I have looked in the mirror every morning and asked myself: "If today were the last day of my life, would I want to do what I am about to do today?" And whenever the answer has been "No" for too many days in a row, I know I need to change something."

--Steve Jobs

Those are wise words to live by. Very wise. Use wisdom. If your dream was to backpack across Europe for a year without a job, well, that might not be the wisest dream to live out. Be responsible. Bills still need to be paid, and groceries still need to be bought. Now, if you are debt free, and have a multimillion dollar money making idea, then by all means, *go for it!* What are you waiting for?

The greatest gift you can give back to God is being who He created you to be. He was particular in what gifts he placed inside of you. The world awaits.

Men. Go seize and conquer.

Follow The Leader

I'm about to write about one of my favorite things: my kids. I, Kirsten Hart, am crazy head-over-heels in love with my two boys. The simply are amazing. I always hated when people would warn me about upcoming years in the lives of my boys. "Oh, just wait 'till he's two. They're all terrors at two." The two's were wonderful—for both of my boys. "If they're good when they're young, just wait until they're teenagers. Teenagers are rotten." Excuse me negative people, but my teenagers were absolutely delightful, and complete JOYS! So there!

I can't stand negative talkers. If you are a young parent, or don't even have children yet, take heed. Every (and I emphasize *every*) stage of a child's life can be wonderful. Don't listen to people who will discourage you and talk negatively about children or teenagers. Just because they may have messed up with their children rearing does not mean you will, or have to, too. There's my two cents. Well, more like a dime's worth.

Those of us who are parents are given great responsibility. It's amazing how you can go from just husband and wife to all of a sudden having complete responsibility for a brand new life. Books, parents, and friends try to prepare you, but you just have to jump in feet first, and experience it firsthand. No one can fully prepare you. Yet, since Adam and Eve, every brand new parent has had the same experience. You are given a brand new life to love, and mold. Our child's future lays literally in our laps.

I love being a mom. I have loved raising my children in the way I believed was right for them. That's what every good parent tries to do. We want our children to have an even better childhood than we had, and our goal is for our children to live fulfilled and full lives. So how do we do that? How do we help our children discover what their gifts are? How do we take these little lives that God has given us, and help them become who they were created to be? Gently, and with a lot of love and guidance.

There are so many issues that we face as parents, but one of the 'biggies' is discipline. I have heard oh too often, people quote the scripture 'spare the rod, spoil the child' in my life. As if your child, if not whooped on a regular basis, will end up being spoiled rotten. Granted, I don't have my doctorate in Child Development, but at this point in life, I have a married son in the Army, and one in college, so I can give advice in rearing your children at least until the present ages of our sons. I *will* tell of my personal journeys of raising my boys to the ages they are. That much I have experienced. That much I know. Does that sound fair?

I have always had a problem with the 'spare the rod, spoil the child' verse. It just never seemed right to me. In particular, how so many American parents have interpreted this verse. A while ago, I did some of my own investigating, and research into this verse, and its meaning. Would you be surprised to find out that 'spare the rod, spoil the child' is actually a *saying* and *not* scripture? Would it disgust you to think of all the parents that have beaten their children so that they would not end up 'spoiled'? It did surprise me, and it did disgust me.

Parenting Techniques 101: we learn about parenting from how our parents parented us. The good and the bad, we learned from being raised in our households. Just as those that were abused as children largely grow up to be abusers themselves, we somehow tend to continue the legacy given to us by our parents. Why spank? Because that's how *we* were disciplined by our parents. Why did our *parents* spank? Because *their* parents spanked. We learn from past behaviors. We, as parents, do what we learned in our own homes. But does that make it right?

When I became a mom, I never thought about 'will I spank or not'. I was just happy to have my newborn son, and make sure that he was taken care of. I honestly never had to spank our firstborn, Tyler. He always listened, and was unbelievably obedient.

One time, when he was three, we had a church function, and the little ones were in a room watching a movie. I went to the door, and called for Tyler to come. It was time for us to go home. Either he didn't hear me, or he ignored me. He probably didn't hear me. I called for him again, and he still didn't come to the door. Finally I went in and picked him up, and took him out in the hall. I was a bit frustrated that he hadn't come to me right away, and I remember spanking him, and telling him that he needed to listen to me, when I told him to come.

I'll never forget the look on his face. I had instinctively reacted like my parents had with me when I didn't listen. I used to get a spanking, so my Tyler got a spanking. It was kind of an out of body reaction. When I looked at Tyler's face, I saw a completely broken child. I broke something that shouldn't have been broken. I overreacted, and did what my parents would have done, instead of what *I* should have done. He was just watching a movie. I was acting out of frustration instead looking at the whole situation. He didn't deserve a spanking. He just needed me to tell him to please come whenever I call him, and that I understood that the movie was fun to watch. I had used a 'rod' in the wrong sense of the word. Rods weren't meant for hitting in Bible times, they were meant for guiding.

There's a huge difference between a hitting rod, and a guiding rod. It never made sense to me for parents to teach their children 'don't hit', and then they would hit their children in retribution if *they* hit someone. Always seemed like a double standard. '*You're not allowed to hit anyone. Yet I, as your parent can hit you in* response *to you hitting someone else'.* Huh? What? How could scripture teach a double standard?

First of all, I need to correct everyone who quotes 'spare the rod, spoil the child'. Sorry, Charlie, the Bible never says that. The verse that so many refer to when they say 'spare the rod' actually says, "*He who spares the rod hates his son, but he who loves him is careful to discipline him.*" --Prov. 13:24.

Now this verse has been used to prove that hitting a child with a 'rod' is biblical. If the rod is used for hitting, how does one rectify the verse: "*Your rod and your staff, they comfort me.*" --Psalm 23:4? How can a hitting rod also be comforting? I don't know about you, but being spanked was never a comforting experience for me.

Ready for a Hebrew lesson? Ready to possibly change your mind about the biblical hitting rod? You still with me?

First, we must change our mindset from the English language to Hebrew. Some words just don't translate well. We are so accustomed to what words mean in

English that we don't realize that the originally translated Hebrew words could have entirely different meanings. (Quick example: 'There was no room in the INN'. In the Christmas story, we English speakers interpret Inn as a sort of hotel. The actual translation back into the Hebrew: *Inn* is an upper room in a home. The other time that the Hebrew word used for the Inn of the Christmas story refers to the 'Inn' or upper room where Jesus met with his disciples. Interesting, huh! If properly translated to its original meaning, the word Inn referred to in the birth of Jesus was probably the upper room in Joseph's family home. COMPLETELY different than what we have been taught!)

So let's quickly look at the Hebrew word for 'rod' as used in the verse that so many quote in Proverbs 13. The Hebrew word for rod is *shevet*. In the Bible, the rod/shevet is a symbol of authority.

The word for rod in Hebrew is not *makel*, which means stick. Rather it's *shevet*, which is translated rod, branch, and sceptre. The rod was used by the shepherd to safeguard the sheep. Every shepherd of Israel had a rod (shevet) and a staff that were used to guide, protect, and set boundaries for the sheep.

The shepherd used the rod to drive away predators like coyotes and wolves. He didn't use his rod to beat his sheep. Psalm 23 says, "*The Lord is my Shepherd, I shall not want... Your rod and Your staff, they comfort me.*" His rod (shevet) and staff are our comfort when walking through the valley of the shadow of death as he leads us to the green pastures and still waters of eternal life. Young children also need this kind of sacrificial shepherding from their parents so that they don't stray into paths where they could be injured or destroyed.

This can't be right? Well, I did my research from Israeli, Jewish sources. If anyone knows what the Hebrew interpretations of the Old Testament should be, it would be Jewish people. Agreed?

So how have we strayed so far away from what the scriptures meant as a guideline for raising our children? I believe that we are inadvertently lazy creatures. Spanking take less time, and is easier for a parent, than sitting down with our children and explaining to them what course, or path is better for them than the actions they took that *led* to needing discipline.

Discipline isn't defined by hitting or spanking. The word discipline is also used in regards to athletes. I love this definition of discipline: *Training expected to produce a specific character or pattern of behavior, especially training that produces moral or mental improvement.* Isn't that a much more positive viewpoint to disciplining our children? 'Training' takes a *lot* of effort and time. Hitting is quicker, training is longer, but the results are so much richer, and long lasting.

Why all the talk of spanking and 'rods'? We, as parents and leaders of our children have an obligation to guide them in the way they should go. Throughout their years in our homes, if we started to incorporate a rod of *guidance* and *training,* then I believe we could see our children grow into the fulfilled people God created them to be.

The Shepherd's rod in Psalms guided the sheep to safety, and kept them from harm. The Shepherd could see what the sheep couldn't, and he was always looking out for them. We as parents are given our 'sheep' for just a few years. It is vital that we train them in God's ways, and to encourage them to discover their own dreams and futures.

Proverbs 22:6 gives some other great parenting advice: *"Train up a child in the way he should go, Even when he is old he will not depart from it."*

There have been so many interpretations of this verse in regards to Biblical parenting. Most of the time it is roughly interpreted in the church as *'Train up a child in the way I know he should go: to church, to obey me, and to do what I say'.* Bible believing parents believe that this verse justifies their laws and rules. Now don't get me wrong, I'm not promoting a 1960's out-there Hippie 'far-out' version of parenting.

Instead of interpreting the above verse as a tough disciplining, 'I can tell you what you should do all the time because I'm your parent, and I'm training you the way I want you to go' view, let's once again look at what the actual Hebrew language version means. The Hebrew emphasizes that a parent's training must be based on knowing their child. The word "train," the Hebrew *chanak,* has as its primary meaning, "train, instruct, initiate," and it can also mean, "to dedicate, throttle or discipline." In this verb we see the primary responsibility. Parents are to train and teach their children to be under God's control. Since children are trusts from God, parents need to dedicate their children to God and be dedicated themselves to the training process.

"In the way he should go." The original Hebrew text is actually much stronger than this and literally reads, "according the measure of his way." It is spelled out for us with the words "his way." The Hebrew text has the personal pronoun attached to the noun "way." It reads, "his way" and not simply "in the way he should go." "Way" is the Hebrew *derek*, "way, road, journey, manner." It was used of (1) a way, path, journey, course of action, (2) mode, habit, manner as a customary experience or condition.

We need to recognize that God, in his sovereignty, has a plan, a course he wants each child to follow. Secondly, we know that every child has a specific make up as an individual with certain abilities, talents, and tendencies—a particular bent. *Derek* is from the verb *darak*, "to tread, march". *Darak* was often used metaphorically of launching something as in the bending of a bow in order to launch an arrow. While *derek* does not have this specific meaning, the use of the verb form provides us with an interesting illustration considering the nature of children according to inheritance factors and as God has designed them.

The *way* our children *go* now makes such a beautiful picture of how we should parent. Our parental role is to raise these children that God gave us, and to find what God has placed inside of them. To help them discover their talents, gifts, and dreams, and to encourage them to walk their lives in fulfillment of who they were created to be.

Apply every chapter of this book to the lives of your children. What are they good at? What do they love to do? What talents have others noticed in them? It is truly the greatest gift we can give to the next generation: To have them walk in the path God designed for them.

Our oldest son, Tyler has always been a natural born leader. We traveled on the road for many years as a family, and it never ceased to amaze me when I saw Tyler rounding up other church kids (that were complete strangers to him until that Sunday morning or evening), and he'd organize everyone into an activity or game. And this was when he was just little! Even the older kids would listen to him.

We used to have Tyler and Ryan come up on stage and sing with us every service. They were stinking adorable. It was the highlight of our concert. When Tyler entered middle school, he took up the trumpet. He had great natural abilities. Horn players would comment on what great tone and control he had for being so young. We would feature him with a trumpet solo every concert. Fun times.

When Tyler's voice started changing, it wasn't so

fun for him to sing with us. The songs that we had sung together even throughout the middle school years didn't work with his voice any more. At that point, I didn't want to make him uncomfortable, and to push him into singing with us. I felt, as his mother, that it was time for him to decide if *he* still wanted to sing with us. He told us that he was always incredibly nervous before concerts, and that it wasn't something that he thoroughly enjoyed. That comment was a red flag. I felt that from that point on, if we *made* him be a part of our concerts, we would be pushing him away.

His trumpet playing continued until I home schooled him in 10th and 11th grades. When he reentered public school for his senior year, he showed no interest in playing trumpet, but rather was quite interested in being an excellent student, and maintaining a 4.0 GPA. Tyler graduated 12th out of his class of over 500 students. He had found his gift— academia! We had an incredibly gifted student on our hands. A natural born leader *and* a very intelligent young man.

Now where did he get that from? Dave and I did OK in high school and college. I don't think either of us were personally driven to get 4.0 GPA's. We were both more involved in the music departments. Now we have this child who excelled in learning. I would study *hours* for a high school exam and get a B. Tyler wouldn't study at *all* and he'd walk away with an A+. Unbelievable.

We didn't push him to continue in our personal

path of music. We encouraged him to do what he loved and enjoyed, and to be who *he* was created to be. Dave had to give up his dream of him singing and touring with us a family, but our dreams aren't the same dreams that God gives our children. We have to let go of what we desire them to be, and open ourselves to the possibilities of God's completely different direction for their lives. The reward? Seeing our children thrive. There's nothing better.

Our Tyler is a married soldier serving at Fort Bragg, in North Carolina. Did I *ever* think he would be bound for the military? Nope. Did I *ever* think my trumpet-playing baby boy would be wearing fatigues and jumping out of airplanes? No way. But his natural leadership abilities and uncommon intelligence will get him far in his military career. He has found his *way.* There isn't anything more rewarding in this entire world.

What about our other son? He is at a special Media Broadcasting School, working in TV, and excelling at his calling. I did the same thing when his voice changed. No forcing him to sing with mom and dad. There were some years where he didn't really sing at all. That was OK. He is discovering his *own* gifts and talents.

Granted, my boys may end up in completely different careers than what they are interested in now, but the fact that they are enjoying life, and fulfilled in their walk is what is vitally important.

I believe God parents us the same way with his

'guiding rod'. He doesn't want to 'whack' us into a new chapter of our lives by making our reinvention harsh, hard, and horrible. He loves us. He desires to guide us in the direction he created for us.

I hope that this chapter will give you encouragement as a parent. Am I claiming to be the perfect parent and to have all the answers? No. Parenting can be life's toughest job. It can also be utterly rewarding. You make that choice. You choose how to parent your children. Make the decision to be an encourager, and commit to the decision to help them discover God's individual calling on their lives. May they follow your guidance and leadership into dreams and visions for their futures.

OLD DOGS AND THEIR TRICKS

You know the saying, 'you can't teach an old dog new tricks'. I 'beg' to differ. We recently had to put down our wonderful Shetland Sheepdog, Dutchess. We bought Dutchess just a month after we purchased our first Sheltie (short for Shetland Sheepdog) puppy, Noah.

Dave and I had fun searching for just the right breed for our family. When we were first married, we bought Cuddles (I believe I mentioned her earlier in the book). Cuddles was supposed to be part Miniature Poodle and part something else. It's been too long, and I can't remember. While we thought she would look one way, she ended up looking more mutt and part dachshund complete with Yoda ears. I learned for the first time through raising Cuddles, that canines could have two separate fathers in the same litter. I had never known that before. Apparently Cuddles' mother was a tad promiscuous in the neighborhood.

We had Cuddles, and then when we were pregnant with Tyler, we brought Cookie into the family. We heard from friends, that sometimes the 'single child aka first dog' in a family can get quite jealous of a newborn baby, and it is better that they have a companion. That weekend Cookie was adopted.

Cookie (a fawn colored Cocker Spaniel) and Cuddles did well with each other their first few years. Then it happened. Our two dominant females started vying for the 'top girl' position. They started fighting. At this time, Ryan was a newborn, and two aggressive female dogs was not the ideal environment for a baby. We had a problem.

We took both dogs to the veterinarian, and asked if there was a solution to the fighting. He told us we would have to make one less submissive by letting one of the females always "win" the fights. I wasn't up to the challenge. Sweet Cookie went to another family. May she rest in peace. I hope she had a great life.

May Cuddles rest in peace, too. Just a year after Cookie went to live with another family, Cuddles stayed with a 'host family' while we moved to Colorado. We called back to the family to have Cuddles shipped to us, only to learn that Cuddles had decided that she wanted to live on her own out in the farms of Ohio. (That's what I like to believe). She had run off. Hopefully she lived her life chasing cows and chickens until she entered doggie heaven.

With one additional mishap of an adoption (mean Princess), oh, and the two sibling puppies that were going to be put to death at the shelter that we ended up giving to a great loving family, we took the challenge of finding the right dog and breed for our family.

We were touring on the road, and stopped at a local dog show. The dogs that were in the main ring that afternoon were all Shetland Sheepdogs. They were stunningly beautiful creatures. We chatted with a breeder, and liked everything we heard about the breed. Loyal, great with kids, superior in their intelligence, not fragile. It sounded like Shelties and the Harts were a great match.

When we settled down off the road, we set out to find a Sheltie breeder. We found a champion breeder about forty minutes away. And she just happened to have a litter of puppies available.

Maybe it's a 'girl thing', but I absolutely love puppy breath. There's just something so tenderly wonderful about it. Puppy breath and puppy kisses=perfection. We brought our boys with us and played with the 6-week old puppies. One kept grabbing our attention. That little one became ours. We named him Noah. We were living in Tulsa, Oklahoma at the time, and had been in a summer-long drought. The day we went to pick Noah up, it was raining. Thus, the name Noah. Cute, huh.

We knew the benefits of having two dogs, but we had just put new carpeting in our home, and didn't want to have to potty train two puppies at once. Noah trained in record time, and we were feeling that there was still another addition that our family needed. We called up our Sheltie breeder to see if there were any more puppies available. She had sold all of Noah's siblings, but, she said, she had one very sweet female named Rose that was about three months old. She was older, and we were thinking about a younger puppy, but we went to meet this little Rose.

It was love at first lap sitting. We brought both boys, as well as Noah, to meet this potential family member. Would she fit? She ran into the room, nudged and sniffed Noah, and then sat right in my lap. She had never been with little children, and within minutes was licking the faces of our boys. Done deal. Rose was in.

We all put in our votes as to Rose's new name, and we came up with Dutchess. Dutchess it was. The name fit perfectly. Our family was complete.

The breeder we first talked to about Shelties was right, they are an incredibly smart breed. I'm not a 'dog whisperer', but if I were a betting woman, I would bet that Dutchess and Noah perfectly understood the English language, and communicated with us in near-human ways. Such intelligence. Sadly Noah passed at the age of six, and Dutchess lived eleven wonderful, full years. The day that we took her to the veterinarian office to have her euthanized because of extreme muscle atrophy, it was as if one of my own flesh and blood children was being put down. It was horrible.

We didn't teach Dutchess a host of fancy dog tricks, although I believe she could have learned any and all tricks dogs perform. She was, though, always learning new words. She had a remarkable capacity to understand things we said. How do I know she knew what we were saying? Her eyes. She was very expressive, and could communicate so well. I believe that if Dutchess had lived beyond the age of eleven, she would have continued learning more and more.

See, you really can teach an old dog new tricks. Don't believe what others say. Are you an old dog? No, not are you a *canine*, but are you someone that perhaps society thinks is past the age of learning something new? You can prove them wrong, just like our Dutchess did.

We recently flew into the Phoenix airport. As we were descending the escalator down to baggage claim, I looked up at the digital advertising board. The University of Phoenix's advertisement showed an elderly woman in her cap and gown, smiling with a diploma in hand. Next to her photo, it read, 'Eloise Hunter, Age 93, University of Phoenix Graduate'. I smiled. That was awesome. How inspirational. If a 93 year-old woman can go to college and graduate with her diploma in hand, what's to stop *me* from achieving my dreams?

No matter what your age, God still has great dreams and plans for your life. Perhaps you never completed your college degree, and thought it was too late to go back and finish. Think about Eloise! If she can do it, you can do it! What did you always want to accomplish, yet thought, 'Oh, it's too late for me'? I'm here to tell you it's *never* too late!

If you woke up this morning, then God still has plans for you. If everything you were supposed to accomplish on earth were over, God would call you home to be with him. He would gladly receive you at the Golden Gates, and say, "Well done, good and faithful servant". Did you wake up on this side of eternity this morning? Then you still have life to live, and 'tricks' to learn! You're not done!

As I mentioned earlier, my absolute favorite Bible character is Moses. He makes me smile. I love his relationship with God. Moses would complain, God would listen. God would speak, Moses would listen and obey. They worked well together.

I'm sure Moses, at age 80, looked as if he was an 'Old Dog Who Couldn't Learn A New Trick'. We almost forget that Moses was *second* in command of all of Egypt. He was a ruler. A prince by adoption, and a mighty warrior. He lived a prestigious life. Yet, at the age of 40, he became a mere sheep herder. Granted, he was an incredibly strong and intelligent Shepherd, but a Shepherd, none the less.

Could you imagine how hard it must have been? He went from the finest luxuries and living in the palace to roughing it in the desert and living in a tent. I wonder if Moses thought his dreams were gone. That there was nothing left for him to do in his world. That he indeed was an 'old dog who couldn't learn a new trick'.

God had other plans in mind. I believe that before Moses was even *born,* God had his future all planned out. God knew what Moses was capable of, and all of those years in the palace combined with his forty years in the desert perfectly prepared him to take charge of the Israelites, and be their new Desert Leader. The perfect combination of his previous eighty years of life. Moses had eighty years of preparation for his ultimate vocation! He most certainly *did* learn some new tricks, and he led a whole nation (almost, it was actually Joshua who led them) into to the Promised Land.

Perhaps you feel as if you are Moses stuck out in the desert. Your past career is over. You have peaked. It's all lifeless from here out. You're on the downhill ride. It's been years since anything remotely 'reinvented' has happened in your life. Be ready, God might just have your most productive years just around the corner. Everything you have done in your life previous to this moment may have just been your preparation. Live with expectancy.

What if you've lived your whole life, and your dream and vision has *never* come in to reality? You've hit retirement age, and *still* you're waiting for your big break. Have no fear. If Colonel Sanders can do it, you can, too.

First off, there is nothing, I repeat, *nothing* like having a bucket of KFC's original recipe chicken, and taking it up in the mountains to eat with your family. The best. Slap some coleslaw, mashed potatoes and gravy, and biscuits into the picture, and you have the perfect Mountain Feast. I want some right now. I want some mountains *and* Kentucky Fried Chicken. And I want to eat it sitting beside a rushing mountain stream, please. Does that not sound *perfect?*

I am always intrigued by a good life story. The story of Colonel Sanders does not disappoint.

Harland Sanders lived a rough childhood. His father died when he was only six years old. He had to drop out of school to help his mother take care of his younger sister and brother, and in particular to cook for them. He started in the workforce at age ten! He worked various odd jobs until the age of forty. When he was forty, he opened a Shell gas station, where travelers could also grab something to eat inside the station. I love that kind of entrepreneurial thinking!

He eventually moved his food business to a restaurant across the street. Only after a few years of selling his fried chicken in the restaurant, it had to be shut down, because the new highway through town needed that land. When his restaurant was forced into closing, and at the age of 65, the only money he had coming in was his $100 social security check. He started anew. Being the ultimate entrepreneur, He started traveling by car to different restaurants and cooked his fried chicken on the spot for restaurant owners. If the owner liked the chicken, they would enter into a handshake agreement to sell the Colonel's chicken. Legend has it that Colonel Sanders heard 1,009 "no's" before he heard his first "yes".

With 1,009 veto's, I think I would have given up.

He was turned down one-thousand and nine times before his chicken was accepted once! The deal was that for each piece of chicken the restaurant sold, Sanders would receive a nickel. The restaurant would receive packets of Colonel's secret herbs and spices in order to avoid them knowing the recipe. By 1964, Colonel Sanders had 600 franchises selling his trademark chicken. HE WAS 74 YEARS OLD! At this time, he sold his company for $2 million dollars but remained as a spokesperson.

Now if that story doesn't light your fire, your wood is wet! Amen?

Let's say you plan to retire at 65. Let's also say that you will live to the ripe age of 95. (Work with me here, folks...with good health, exercise, and eating well, 95 is a viable option!) You could have a completely new career for another THIRTY years of your life! Isn't that exciting?

I want to keep reinventing myself and learning new 'tricks'. I don't ever want my life to grow stale. If I keep at writing and speaking, and I live to my goal age of

100, I still have 52 years to create! Just think of all the books I could write in 52 years!

Be open to what God has for you. Don't reminisce about what *was,* or what *never was.* Dream new dreams. Create new goals. Dig deep into your Creator DNA. What new ventures will you accomplish? What has God designed for you to do in your life that hasn't yet been done.

If our Dutchess could have lived a human lifespan, I believe she could have learned to actually *speak* the human language. Oh, she would have been capable. Don't believe me? I was her *mother.* I know these things!

Now you go brainstorm on what you want to do with the rest of your life while I go buy some Kentucky Fried Original Recipe chicken legs. 'Cause that's all I can think about right now.

THERE'S A GREAT BIG BEAUTIFUL TOMORROW

I have two favorite rides in Tomorowland at Walt Disney World's Magic Kingdom. I'm sure some of you would guess one of them to be Space Mountain. Nope. You're wrong. My husband and I were at Disney World last week for a Christian music conference. You know how those work, though, don't you? A few conference sessions. Play. A few more conference sessions. Play some more. And play we DID! We had a blast together. (And I guess it would be proper to mention that we did actually have some musical takeaways from the conference).

"Let's go on Space Mountain!" my cute hubby suggested. Not my favorite. Trying to be a supportive wife, we got in line (a very short one thankfully), and boarded our pint-sized space rocket. I made sure that my 'security bar' was as tight as possible across my lap. As I braced myself for the upward ascent, I noticed all the teeny small children on the ride. *I really should be braver. Should, but I'm not.* I never have been a fan of roller coasters, although, *yes*, I realize this is a comparatively 'baby' roller coaster.

Relax I kept telling myself. *Re-lax. You're a grown woman. This ride is not going to injure you. Relax and try to enjoy this ride. Be a big girl.*

I didn't feel so horribly bad when, upon ascending to the top of the indoor coaster, we abruptly stopped short, and I heard my husband groan deeply when the security bar deeply jarred the insides of his lower abdomen. *See, I knew this ride was dangerous.*

I closed my eyes and braced my feet against the little foot rests in front of me. We twisted and turned, climbed and plummeted. And yes, I did make it out alive. Barely.

"I don't think I ever need to ride that again," I told my husband. He confided to me that his neck and back were hurting after that initial jolt we received. Whew. Of course I felt sorry for him, but I was also slightly relieved that I didn't have to 'journey to space' again. Now if in the future we have grandsons that want to ride Space Mountain, I suppose I will have to put my 'big girl panties' on and pretend to enjoy it.

Now, you wanna know my *favorites?* I, yes I, am proud and not ashamed to admit that I love the

People Mover. Granted, I realize that the People Mover really doesn't fall into the category of an official 'ride'. It's pretty much a monorail without a roof. But on a really hot day at Disney, you can enjoy some air conditioning and nice cool breezes upon the 'Mover'. It's relaxing. It's for old people. It's one of my favorites. Be nice.

My other favorite, you ask? Why, that would be one of the oldest and most famous Walt Disney-personally-created rides, the Carousel Of Progress. It. Is. Wonderful. It's another one of those not-have-to-wait-in-a-long-line rides. OK, well, again, this isn't necessarily a *ride,* although you do move in it. The audience moves *around* the stage. Pure genius.

An interesting fact about the Carousel Of Progress: It was created by Walt Disney for the GE (General Electric) Pavilion for the 1964-1965 World's Fair. If you've read my book, Baby Girl Murphy, you'll know that I was conceived from two people that worked at the Kodak Pavilion for that same World's Fair. I'm thinking that perhaps while I was still but a wee zygote, my birth mother went on the Carousel Of Progress, and that is why I love the ride so deeply. I fell in love with that song while in utero. It all makes sense now.

A few years ago when we 'rode' The Carousel Of Progress, we had our two sons with us. We were on the very last scene. Do you remember it? The family is in the future, and Grandma is playing a video game. The scene is set at Christmas time. It's cute. I chuckled.

The song 'There's A Great Big Beautiful Tomorrow' played. The animatronic family sang along. The audience didn't move. We were supposed to have moved to the "please gather your things and depart from the ride" section. The animatronic family sang again. And again. The ride was stuck, and we were 'fortunate' to hear that wonderful song over and over again. Fun family memories. We still talk and laugh about it today.

Perhaps the ride is getting a tad old. It *is* two years older than I am, and I'm getting old myself. When my husband and I rode it last week, we were yet again blessed to have a 'double portion' of the great song during one scene. It was the scene where the wife is wallpapering the 'new' RUMPUS ROOM. It makes me smile just writing it now. Remember that scene? Remember the song? It's a classic, and since I knew I was going to write this chapter today, the song has been stuck in my head non-stop. That's OK. It's a great song with a great positive message.

I wanted to end this book with the last chapter based on this song. Feel free to sing along, my friends. If you grew up going to Disney like I did, it should bring back special memories. OK, warm up those vocal chords. Mi-Mi-Mi-Mi-Mi. Ready, set, sing!

There's a great big beautiful tomorrow

173

Shining at the end of ev'ryday
There's a great big beautiful tomorrow
And tomorrow's just a dream away

Man has a dream and that's the start
He follows his dream with mind and heart
And when it becomes a reality
It's a dream come true for you and me

So there's a great big beautiful tomorrow
Shining at the end of ev'ryday
There's a great big beautiful tomorrow
Just a dream away

Are those not the best words ever? Well, to be honest, It's A Small World is a close second. Interestingly enough, both songs were written by the Sherman Brothers, who were good friends of Walt Disney. Just call me a walking book of Disney trivia. You're very welcome. I've got more if you want to contact me personally. Perhaps we could find all of the 'hidden Mickey's' around the Magic Kingdom and all the parks. Let's go!

"Fun song, Kirsten, but I'm still waiting for *my* dreams to come true. You may have found your personal 'reinvention', but I'm *still waiting. My* dreams seem so very far away."

So what do you do in these middle times? How do

you face each new day knowing that what you have envisioned for your life is still just a *dream*. A dream that is so far from your actual reality?

The Christian singing group, TRUTH (directed by Roger Breland) had a song out titled, 'Keep Believing'. (My husband sang with this group. Just wanted to tell you that fact *again*). The chorus to the song has these words:

> *Keep Believing*
> *In what you know is true*
> *Keep Believing*
> *You know the Lord will see you through.*
>
> *When troubles rise in your life*
>
> *And you don't know what to do*
>
> *You'll be fine*
>
> *If you just*
>
> *Keep Believing.*

Those are great words. Even though you can't see what God is doing in your life at this very moment, keep holding on. Keep believing. Keep preparing.

Perhaps you feel that the Lord has revealed to you a reinvention for your life, but it hasn't come in to reality yet. But that idea, vision, has been planted in your *heart,* and you know that you know God has revealed this to you. What do you *do* in the meantime? You prepare.

I can remember how excited we were when we

found out that we were pregnant with our first baby. We weren't making much money at the time, but we did our best to get everything we needed for our future newborn. We took the nine months to slowly store up all of our needed supplies. Each month we would buy a little more as we got the nursery set up.

We were living in Tulsa, Oklahoma at the time. I've always been quite the discount and thrifty shopper. It's my female form of game hunting. There's nothing like the Thrill of The Hunt—Thrift Store Edition. I love thrift stores. Especially really good ones that don't have that typical *scent.*

My husband and I found some great thrift stores in Tulsa, and were happily surprised to find such bountiful supplies of nearly-new baby clothes. To find baby clothes with the tags still on them in brand new condition? As if I, myself shot down the season's Trophy Elk. Yep, that wonderful.

We saw signs of an upcoming HALF-OFF sale. Now that's talking my language. Half-off of *thrift store* prices? Almost as delightful as a hot fudge brownie sundae. My husband (bless him for putting up with me) and I had our game plan. The thrift stores (there were two with the same half off sale that day) would open their doors at 7am. Our plan? To be the last ones in the store the night before. Right before closing, we would take all the baby clothes that we wanted to purchase the next morning, and place them together in an obscure part of the store. (Be nice. We weren't making a lot of money back then, and we had to revert to extreme measures.) That way, when the doors opened in the morning, we were off to grab our loot, and be *outta there!*

We did it. We divided to conquer. We each had a vehicle. We each had a plan. We each had to accomplish the goal at hand. Run, grab, and buy.

You, my friend, would not believe the numbers of people that stood at those thrift store doors the next morning waiting to grab their discounted treasures. My goodness. And these people were determined. Thrift store door openings on ½ off days are not for the faint of heart. This was full-on battle mode. I had a mission. *YES, SIR. HOOAH!*

I used my pregnant state and mask of innocence to make it to the front of the line. Pregnant and sweet they all thought. Oh, if they only knew. There she was. The woman with the key. Wait. Wait. Calm down. Wait. And...*GO!*

Still pregnant but innocent no more, I ran to my hidden loot. It was all there. The plan was succeeding. *Roger. Over and Out.*

I left all the innocents grazing through the racks. All the really cute newborn boy clothes were on their way outta there. Ya snooze ya lose. Mama bear was making sure that her baby cub would be dressed *fine.* Fine and on the cheap!

Sound impressive? My husband an equal warrior. Two thrift store missions completed. Back and home in thirty minutes. Upon arriving back at our apartment, we dumped all our loot on the couch, and promptly counted up how much we had saved in our double quest. That was a *good* morning. That was wise preparation for our child.

Dave and I were doing what it took to get ready for our baby. You need to get ready for *your* 'baby'. You want your dream to come, right? Then start preparing for it as if it's already on its way.

Speak positive words, as if your answer is just around the corner. Be active in preparing for your vision to come alive. If we had just sat watching TV for the nine months prior to Tyler's birth, we could never have taken care of him! Our 'dream' would have arrived, but we wouldn't have known what to do, or how to take care of our newborn son.

I remember reading the book 'What To Expect When You're Expecting' as if it were my life support. I needed to soak up every last tidbit of information, so that I was as prepared as I could be to take care of a newborn child. Are you doing everything to prepare for your vision or dream to come true? Perhaps God has your dream ready, but you haven't done your prep work. If God dropped your completed vision in your lap right now, it would die, because you haven't stored up your supplies. You weren't ready.

I want you living in daily expectation. Believe that your future holds more than your past. Keep birthing new ideas, and preparing for their arrival. Know everything there is to know about the new career field you dream about entering. Seek, find, and learn. Connect with those in your dream career now. Learn from them. How did they get to where there are now? What were the proper steps? Write every bit of information down. Read and re-read it all. Soak up every bit of knowledge you can. When it's time for God to reinvent you, your 'thank you' to him can be that you had done everything in your power to be worthy of what he has for you.

I believe in you. God believes in you. I believe you were created with amazing gifts and abilities. God *knows* you were created with amazing gifts and abilities.

Live your life full and fulfilled. Live everyday as if it were your last on Earth. Don't sit and wish for what never happened. Go out and seize the day. Check off every item from your bucket list. When you've lived every last second of your purpose here on Earth, and as you breathe your last breath, I pray that you will smile, and know that you *did* it. You lived the life God intended for you. Smile, relax, and move on to your next journey. Someday I'll meet you there. (Let me reach 100 first). We'll have all of eternity to chat. I would love for you to look me up. Let's get together. Then you can tell me all of your life's adventures, reinventions, and how you lived every last second of your life full of anticipation for what God was going to do next.

We think there is so much for us to do here on Earth. We have no idea the plans and dreams God has ready for us in Heaven! That is our ultimate reinvention! This is just our rehearsal!

' Well done, good and faithful servant! You have been faithful with a few things; I will put you in charge of many things. Come and share your master's happiness! '

-- Jesus

ABOUT THE AUTHOR

Author, speaker, and singer Kirsten Hart has been able to travel with some of America's premier Christian singing groups, including Re-Creation, Eternity, The Spurrlows, FRIENDS (the back-up group for Grammy Award winner Larnelle Harris), The Richard Roberts TV Singers, as a Praise and Worship Leader for International Crusades, and on TBN's This Is Your Day telecast. Since moving to Branson, Missouri, she has been a part of DINO Kartsonakis' Christmas Spectacular Show, as well as his Tribute To The Titanic production.

She has had the amazing opportunity to sing on television, in hundreds of churches, and as part of international crusades. She has shared her heart before thousands. She also counts it a privilege to have sung for FOCUS ON THE FAMILY and COMPASSION INTERNATIONAL events, Camp Meetings, Statewide Conventions, and more.

Kirsten has spoken in churches and for Women's Ministry Events across the country for the past twenty-five years.

SMALL GROUP CHAPTER QUESTIONS

CHAPTER 1: A LIFELONG JOURNEY

What are you still waiting for in your life?

Would you have been able to walk through the circumstances and situations Esther did? Was her reinvention to 'go in to' the King worth the humiliation? What would have happened to her if she did not 'please' the King that night?

Are you willing to walk though danger and humiliation for a greater purpose? Is it worth it to you to reach your goal? Esther was reinvented into the Queen, but not without having sex with the King first. Was that a fair trade? Too large of a gamble?

Have you walked through personal hardships, yet the end result was worth it all? Would you do it all again, knowing the end result?

What's the longest you have waited for a promise to come true?

If you knew that in twenty years, you would have all the wealth and prominence you could ever want, could you patiently wait out 7,300 days? Are you patient by nature? Does patience come easily to you, or do you want immediate results?

What is your dream for your future. Spell it out. Verbalize it. What is keeping you from attaining that dream? Time, relationships, finances?

Have you ever created your own Ishmael (child born out of man misinterpreting God's plan and timetable)? How did you create this 'misinterpretation'? How does one determine when something happens by God's perfect timing, versus our own. What is the difference? Why can't we help move things along for God? Is it that bad/wrong? What was the 'Ishmael' you created?

Have you ever waited what seemed like forever for your 'Isaac'? What did it feel like when that promise finally came true? Why is it important not to rush God's timetable? And *why* isn't God on *our* timetable? (That's the million dollar question!)

Chapter 2: Whistle While You Work

What activity invigorates you?

What do you look forward to?

What is it that when you 'become so immersed that time speeds up and you lose yourself in the present moment'?

What job/work activity makes you feel 'authentic' (the essence of who you are down deep)?

On a scale of 1-10, how connected is your spirit/soul to your work or vocation?

Do you consider what you're doing right now to make money a job or a career? What's the difference between a job and a career?

If you could do a certain job/career for free, just because you love it so, what would you do?

What's your life's calling? Are you who you always wanted to be?

CHAPTER 3: Uphill Both Ways

What did your parents do as their vocation? Did they seem to enjoy work? What about your grandparents? Was it laborious for them, or something they looked forward to?

How did your parent's view of work affect you as a child? Has it affected you as an adult? Inspired you? Made you view a job as something hard or enjoyable?

Did you ever sell products (Girl Scout cookies, etc.) as a child? Did you enjoy it? Were you rewarded for your hard work?

What is the worst thing you had to sell? As a child? As an adult? Your favorite thing to sell? Are you a natural 'salesman'?

How have your early views of having a job or career affected your current job/career?

Is a career more of a God-calling, or is it a vehicle to make money?

187

Have you ever had what you thought was a great money making idea? What is it? How did you come up with the idea? Have you ever tried to make it work, as an actual product? Have other people (friends, family members, etc.) agreed that it was a great idea worth pursuing?

What product out in the market today could you improve on? Are you an ideas person that can always think of new and innovative products?

CHAPTER 4: Firemen And Ballerinas

What did you always want to be when you were younger? Do you know what your spouse wanted to be?

Did you grow up to be what you thought you would be when you were in elementary school?

What were the dream jobs of your friends when you were little?

Why do you think we choose different career paths than what we wanted to do when we were younger?

Do you know anyone that went on to be exactly what they said they were going to be?

Why do vocation dreams change as we grow older?

Do you believe that your personal career calling was already mapped out for you by God while you were still in your mother's womb? If the answer is "yes", why do you think it takes so many of us so long to discover what we are meant to do?

If you could snap your fingers, and immediately reinvent your vocation, would you? What would you change it to?

Name your top five abilities:

Name the top five areas of work that you're *not* good at:

What vocation would you *never* choose?

At this point in your life, can you say, "I am walking in complete fulfillment of who I was created to be."?

What is keeping you from walking in complete fulfillment of your calling?

CHAPTER 5: No Talent Tillie And Tom

Did you grow up in a positive environment?

Were your parents verbally abusive or encouraging?

Did you hear life-giving words, or were you beaten down verbally?

Can you see the effects of your upbringing in your life today?

Did the words your parents spoke to you influence the career path you have today?

Do you come from a line of successful people? Define successful. Define unsuccessful.

How has your upbringing influenced how you parent our own children? Have you followed in their footsteps, or did you do a complete 180?

Did your parents steer you into a particular career?
Did you feel forced to follow in their footsteps, or
obey their wishes?

Have you ever felt like you were a No Talent Tillie or
Tom? Why do you believe you have felt that way?
How can you change that mindset?

Dig a bit in your Bible. What does God say about who
you are? Look up these verses:

Jeremiah 29:1
John 1:12
Galatians 3:26
I Peter 2:10
Ephesians 3:16-19
Jeremiah 31:3
Zephaniah 3:17
I John 3:1

Chapter 6: The Secret Ingredients

Do you like to cook or bake? Just cook? Just bake?

What is your most requested recipe?

What do you enjoy making over and over again?

Are you one that has a secret recipe that you don't share? What is it?

What do you *love to do*?

What is your passion? What are you passionate about?

What are you naturally good at?

Do you know people who think they are literally 'god at nothing'? How does thinking coincide with God's word?

When you read this chapter, did you come up with a list of 'things you are good at'? Verbally share your top five.

What aspects of your current job do you love? Which do you loathe?

What activity makes you completely lose track of time, because you are completely enjoying it?

Did you ask your friends what they thought you were good at? What did they say? Ask your small group friends the same question.

What have you secretly dreamed of doing with your life?

CHAPTER 7: Negative Nellie And Ned

Are your friends on the whole, very upbeat and positive, or slightly depressing.

What kind of people do you usually hang around with?

Do you have a lot of friends, or are they a small circle? What attributes do your closest friends have?

When was the last time you were intellectually challenged by your friends? Spiritually challenged?

Is there someone in your life that always cuts you down, and you always feel horrible after you spend time with them? Why are they still your friend?

Do you feel an obligation to be around certain people, even though you know that spiritually and emotionally, they're not good for you?

If you became a Christian in your adult life, did you keep the same friends? Were your non-Christian friends still influential in your life? Were you chastised for becoming a Christian, or did they support your decision?

Who do you need to filter from being an influence in your life? Can you? Is that too difficult to do?

Have you ever made the decision to distance yourself from someone that was a negative influence in your life? How did they react? Did the friendship continue? How did you *do* the 'distancing'? What would you recommend to someone that needs to distance themselves from this type of person?

Chapter 8: Straight To The Principal's Office

Do you remember the name of your elementary, junior high, or high school principals? Did you have a good relationship with your principals?

Who was the meanest teacher you ever had? Were they mean to everyone, or just you? Why do you think they were that way?

(If) you got in trouble when you were younger, what would you usually get in trouble for? Has that 'trouble making' quality turned out to be a strength of yours, in your adult life?

What was your 'identity' junior high or high school? The funny one? Loud one? Quiet one? Smart one? Artistic one? Athletic one? Trouble maker? Popular one? Involved in sports, theater, band, choir, FHA, academic clubs, student government, or home economics?

How have you transformed from your high school identity? Changed? Stayed the same?

197

Did other people label you as a certain type of student, but deep down you knew you weren't that type of person? If so, how did you break out of that stereotype?

If you have children, what characteristics do you see in them that will transform to be their strengths as adults?

CHAPTER 9: No Thanks But Thank You Though

What have people assumed that you're naturally good at, but that you don't enjoy at all?

Have you ever taken on a job/position/title that you really didn't want, but you did it because you thought it was expected of you?

What are you actually *good* at, yet don't enjoy doing at all? Why do you think this is the case? Why don't you enjoy doing it?

All your life, what have people assumed you're good at?

Have you ever stepped in to help, but dreaded every minute of it? Tell us the scenario.

Do you believe, in a church setting, that people should step up to help in various departments, even though they don't necessarily 'enjoy' it? Is that just part of the Christian servanthood walk?

Does your church hire nursery workers, or rotate parents? What is your stance on that whole situation? Why do you feel the way you do about your opinion?

What is your particular place of joy in a ministry department at your church? Why do you enjoy it? What department would you *not* want to be a part of? Explain why.

Have you ever stepped aside from a church responsibility because you did not feel like it was your place of joy and calling? What did others say/feel about your decisions?

Did you grow up in a family that believed that you step in and help *wherever* there is a need in the church community? Do you believe that way?

How hard is it for you to tell someone "no" in regards to helping in a church setting? Have you ever felt guilt for that 'no'? Is guilt a feeling from God? Where does that guilt come from?

CHAPTER 10: Apple Orchard Lane

What's the name of the street you currently live on? What was your childhood address? Does that address evoke good memories? Do you have a favorite street or road name?

Do you have a dream business? Is it exactly what you're doing right now? If you could snap your fingers and be in your perfect job scenario, what would it be? What would the name of your company be? Why *that* name?

Do you have a great money making idea that hasn't been created yet? What is it? What is holding you back from creating and selling it (if it's an actual product)? What about your spouse? What is one of their great 'we could retire from that money' idea?

What is a product that is available right now, that *you* had the same idea, but "they", 'beat you to it'?

Do you consider yourself a creative person? Do you daily realize that your creative ideas come from God himself, who is the ultimate creator?

If money weren't an option, what product, or business would you create?

CHAPTER 11: Instant Rice

On a scale of 1-10 (ten being really patient), how naturally patient are you? Are you more patient as a Christian believer? Does that help in the 'I want it instantly' situations?

What are you currently waiting for in your life?

What do you want to do, but it seems to be taking so long, you are considering giving it up?

Have you ever seen someone give up on their dreams because the process was too long or difficult? How did their life change, once they gave up? Have you ever given up on something (or someone) because the process was too long?

Do you currently have someone in your life who is *where* you want to be? They have reinvented into what/who *your* goal is, but you aren't there yet. Are they willing to help and mentor you?

Are you able to mentor someone who wants to

actually be where *you* are? How do you encourage your 'apprentice'?

Never burn bridges. How does this statement apply to your life? Are there bridges you have burnt that you now regret? Why did you bun the bridge? Out of anger? Hurt? If you could go back and re-live that situation, what would you change? *Would* you change anything?

CHAPTER 12: Buh-Bye now

Do you know someone that thought they belonged in a certain church ministry department, but it was obvious to everyone else that it wasn't the right fit? How was it handled? Or was it *not* handled?

How would you feel or react if someone approached you, saying that they felt you didn't belong in a certain church ministry?

Have you had positive responses from people about what you feel is your gifting/purpose?

Have family members and loved ones affirmed your giftings and callings?

Do you know anyone that has 'checked out' of normal life to pursue an unrealistic dream? Where are they now? How did their actions affect their family?

Have you struggled and struggled to make your own dream come true, but you're still waiting? Why do you think this is happening? What do you need to change or adjust, or give up in your life?

Would you be happier and filled with more peace if you, yourself, quit trying to reinvent yourself *by* yourself, and instead submit your future to God? Have you completely done that yet?

CHAPTER 13: Dream Capsule

Have you ever participated in putting together a time capsule? If you could do one right now, what would you put in it to represent your life? The town where you live? Your country?

Are you currently involved in something in your life that you never thought would be a part of, but yet now couldn't imagine your life without? (For example, I never thought I would be a speaker, but now I couldn't imagine *not* speaking for events and conferences.)

What are some abilities evident in your life *now* that you never thought would be a part of who you were and now *are*?

Are you waiting for your dream capsule to arrive? Does it feel like it got lost in shipping?

If you could open your perfect life dream capsule, what would it have inside?

Are you wondering why your gifts and dreams are

taking so long to get to you, or do you feel like you are walking in complete fulfilment and purpose?

CHAPTER 14: Let's Hear It For The Boys

*I will ask these questions as if talking to the men reading this book. Girls---you can just skip to the next chapter of questions if you want!

How did you choose your current vocation? Did you feel forced into your line of work? Are you walking in your professional passion?

What influence did your father or parents have on your occupation? Were they encouraging of your vocational choice?

What dream has 'nagged' at you for as long as you can remember, the thing that always pops into your mind no matter how many times you dismiss it?

What fills your thoughts in the quiet moments when you're riding the train or lying in bed? What do you think about incessantly, what captures your imagination? Politics? Spirituality? Relationships?

If time, money, education and any other obstacle was

a non-issue, what kind of work would you choose to do?

What were you doing the last time you totally lost track of time? Have you ever talked to a friend about a topic, a dream, or an aspiration and everything just clicked inside of you, and you felt a surge of excitement throughout your body?

What aspects of your current job do you love, which do you loathe?

What kinds of projects and jobs at work and at home do you get excited about? What kinds do you dread?

How do you interpret this quote by Steve Jobs as it relates to your life? What does this mean to you?

"When I was 17, I read a quote that went something like: "If you live each day as if it was your last, someday you'll most certainly be right." It made an impression on me, and since then, for the past 33 years, I have looked in the mirror every morning and asked myself: "If today were the last day of my life, would I want to do what I am about to do today?" And whenever the answer has been "No" for too many

days in a row, I know I need to change something."
--Steve Jobs

CHAPTER 15: FOLLOW THE LEADER

Were you raised in an environment of encouragement?

Were your parents strict disciplinarians or more laid back in their parenting techniques?

Have you, as a parent, followed in the footsteps of your parents, or changed the methods of how you parent your children?

What are the differences in the way you raise (raised?) your children I comparison to how you were raised?

What is your personal interpretation of 'spare the rod, spoil the child? Have you always believed that this was a passage of scripture?

What were the best things your parents did in raising you? What would you have changed? What did you learn from their parenting techniques?

What are your thoughts on spanking children?

We tell our children not to hit anyone, yet we are free to hit/smack/spank them, is we so choose. Is that a double standard, or our right as parents who discipline?

What is your best parenting advice to parents with young children?

CHAPTER 16: OLD DOGS AND THEIR TRICKS

Are you a dog or cat person? Do you have pets? What kind and how many?

Name an elderly person that is inspirational to you. What is it about his or her life that you admire? What have you learned about life through them?

What do you still have to accomplish in your life? Are you intimidated by your age and abilities?

Have you given up on dreams, because you thought you were 'past your prime'? Do you feel you have the energy and stamina to learn a new trade?

Moses was 80 when he was reinvented to be the leader of Israel. If you could live until the age of 120, what would your life look like? What would you want to accomplish in 120 years? Verbally 'map it out'.

Do you plan to retire at age 65? Are you retired? Does retirement look different to you now, than it did to your grandparents? Are you one to enjoy sitting back, or do you plan to forging ahead at full speed?

CHAPTER 17: THERE'S A GREAT BIG BEAUTIFUL TOMORROW

What is your favorite ride at Disney? Why? Do you have any favorite Disney memories?

What dream are you currently waiting for in your life to come true?

How would you like your life to be reinvented? What do you think are the steps to that next reinvention?

What things did you and your husband (if you're married) do in preparation for your first child? What were some of the necessary items you *had* to purchase in order to be ready?

How would you change your day today, if you knew the dream you have been waiting for would be fulfilled tomorrow? *Would* you change anything?

If you knew the dream and vision God gave you was literally just around the corner, how would you prepare? What still needs to be done? What things in your life would you delete? What would you keep the same?

Who have you connected with that is already doing what you want to be doing? Are you in an apprentice-type relationship with them? Do you currently mentor anyone that wants to be involved in *your* current career or vocation?

We sometimes bring about our own personal reinventions, and sometimes God does the work to reinvent us. Has this happened in your life? What personal reinventions have you walked through? What advice would you give someone who wants to reinvent themselves?

When God reinvents us, it's for a greater purpose. Have you been able to witness and understand why God reinvented your life? Can you share your story?

When I die, I want God to tell me, I lived every day full of purpose, and that I fulfilled my calling on earth. What is burning inside of your soul, that you still feel you have to accomplish while alive in this world?